~ All Time ~

FAMILY FAVORITES™

CASSEROLES & ONE-DISH MEALS

PUBLICATIONS INTERNATIONAL, LTD.

Manufactured in U.S.A.

8 7 6 5 4 3 2 1

ISBN: 0-7853-3220-0

All Time Family Favorites is a trademark of Publications International, Ltd.

All recipes and photographs that contain specific brand names are copyrighted by those companies and/or associations.

DOLE® is a registered trademark of Dole Food Company, Inc.

Louis Rich is a registered trademark of Oscar Mayer Foods Corporation.

Some of the products listed in this publication may be in limited distribution.

Pictured on the front cover: Pace-Setting Enchilada Casserole *(page 104)*.

Pictured on the back cover: Lemon-Garlic Shrimp *(page 54)*.

Microwave Cooking: Microwave ovens vary in wattage. The microwave cooking times given in this publication are approximate. Use the cooking times as guidelines and check for doneness before adding more time. Consult manufacturer's instructions for suitable microwave-safe cooking dishes.

Preparation/Cooking Times: The preparation times in this book are based on the average amount of time necessary to assemble the ingredients before baking, cooking, chilling, freezing or serving. These times do not include the advance preparation and cooking of some ingredients, such as "cooked, peeled and quartered sweet potatoes." When appropriate, simultaneous preparations were taken into account. Preparation of optional ingredients is not included.

— Contents —

— *Homestyle* —

MEATY MEALS

SUCCESS IN A SKILLET

1 bag SUCCESS® Rice
1 teaspoon reduced-calorie margarine
½ cup chopped onion
½ pound chopped turkey-ham
¼ pound sliced fresh mushrooms
½ cup green peas
½ cup chopped tomatoes
¾ teaspoon lemon pepper seasoning
¼ cup water

Prepare rice according to package directions.

Melt margarine in large skillet over medium heat. Add onion; cook and stir until tender. Stir in turkey-ham, mushrooms, peas, tomatoes, lemon pepper and water. Reduce heat to low; simmer until water is absorbed, about 5 minutes. Stir in rice; heat thoroughly, stirring occasionally. *Makes 4 servings*

MEATY MEALS

BEEF BOURGUIGNON

1 boneless beef sirloin steak, ½ inch thick, trimmed, cut into ½-inch pieces (about 3 pounds)
½ cup all-purpose flour
4 slices bacon, diced
3 cups Burgundy wine or beef broth
2 medium carrots, diced
1 teaspoon dried marjoram leaves, crushed
½ teaspoon dried thyme leaves, crushed
½ teaspoon salt
Pepper to taste
1 bay leaf
2 tablespoons vegetable oil
20 to 24 fresh pearl onions
8 small new red potatoes, cut into quarters
8 to 10 mushrooms, sliced
3 cloves garlic, minced

Coat beef with flour, shaking off excess. Set aside.

Cook and stir bacon in 5-quart Dutch oven over medium-high heat until partially cooked. Brown half of beef with bacon in Dutch oven over medium-high heat. Remove with slotted spoon; set aside. Brown remaining beef. Pour off drippings. Return beef and bacon to Dutch oven.

Stir in wine, carrots, marjoram, thyme, salt, pepper and bay leaf. Bring to a boil over high heat. Reduce heat to low. Cover and simmer 10 minutes.

Meanwhile, heat oil in large saucepan over medium-high heat. Cook and stir onions,

potatoes, mushrooms and garlic about 10 minutes. Add to Dutch oven. Cover and simmer 50 minutes or until meat is fork-tender. Discard bay leaf before serving.   *Makes 10 to 12 servings*

CIDER STEW

2 pounds stew beef, cut into 1-inch cubes
2 tablespoons BLUE BONNET® Margarine
¼ cup all-purpose flour
2 cups water
1 cup apple cider
½ cup A.1.® Steak Sauce
2 teaspoons dried thyme leaves
½ teaspoon ground black pepper
1 bay leaf
3 medium potatoes, peeled and cut into 1-inch cubes
3 medium carrots, sliced
1 medium onion, chopped
1 (10-ounce) package frozen cut green beans

In large heavy saucepan, over medium-high heat, brown beef in margarine. Stir in flour. Gradually stir in water, cider and steak sauce. Bring to a boil over high heat; stir in thyme, pepper and bay leaf. Reduce heat to low; cover and simmer 2 hours.

Add potatoes, carrots, onion and beans. Cover and cook 30 minutes or until vegetables are tender. Discard bay leaf before serving.

Makes 6 to 8 servings

Beef Bourguignon

SOUTHWESTERN BEEF AND BEAN LASAGNA

½ **pound extra lean ground beef**
1 **can (16 ounces) pinto beans, drained**
1 **teaspoon cumin seeds** *or* ½ **teaspoon ground cumin**
1 **teaspoon olive oil**
1½ **cups chopped onions**
1 **tablespoon seeded and minced jalapeño pepper**
1 **clove garlic, minced**
4 **cups no-salt-added tomato sauce**
1 **can (4 ounces) diced green chilies, undrained**
2 **teaspoons chili powder**
1 **teaspoon dried oregano leaves**
1 **container (8 ounces) nonfat cottage cheese**
1½ **cups (6 ounces) shredded reduced fat Cheddar cheese, divided**
1 **egg white**
¼ **cup chopped fresh cilantro**
½ **teaspoon salt**
¼ **teaspoon black pepper**
8 **ounces uncooked lasagna noodles**
1 **cup water**

Brown beef in large skillet. Drain off fat. Stir in beans; set aside. Place cumin seeds in large nonstick skillet. Cook and stir over medium heat 2 minutes or until fragrant. Remove from skillet.

In same skillet, heat oil. Add onions, jalapeño and garlic; cook until onions are soft. Add tomato sauce, green chilies, chili powder, oregano and cumin seeds. Bring to a boil; reduce heat. Simmer, uncovered, 20 minutes.

Preheat oven to 350°F. Combine cottage cheese, ½ cup Cheddar cheese, egg white, cilantro, salt and black pepper in medium bowl.

Spray 13 × 9-inch baking pan with cooking spray. Cover bottom with ¾ cup tomato sauce mixture. Place layer of noodles on sauce. Spread half the beef mixture over noodles, then place another layer of noodles on top. Spread cheese mixture over noodles. Spread with remaining beef mixture. Layer with remaining noodles. Pour remaining sauce mixture over all; sprinkle with remaining 1 cup Cheddar cheese. Pour water around edges. Cover tightly with foil. Bake 1 hour and 15 minutes or until pasta is tender. Cool 10 minutes before serving. *Makes 6 servings*

Southwestern Beef and Bean Lasagna

MEATY MEALS

OVERNIGHT CORNBREAD CASSEROLE

- **2 cups frozen mixed vegetables, slightly thawed**
- **1½ cups cubed cooked ham**
- **1 package (8 ounces) cornbread stuffing mix**
- **2 cups milk**
- **3 eggs, lightly beaten**
- **¼ teaspoon salt**
- **¼ teaspoon freshly ground black pepper**
- **½ cup (2 ounces) shredded Cheddar cheese**

In 12 × 8-inch microwavable dish, stir together vegetables, ham and stuffing mix. In medium bowl, combine milk, eggs, salt and black pepper. Pour over cornbread mixture. Cover with plastic wrap; refrigerate overnight or at least 5 hours. Remove plastic wrap; cover with waxed paper. Microwave on HIGH (100% power) 6 minutes. Rotate ¼ turn; microwave on MEDIUM-HIGH (80% power) until wooden pick inserted 1 inch from center comes out clean, 7 to 9 minutes. Sprinkle with cheese. Let stand, covered, 10 minutes. Stir gently before serving.

Makes 4 to 6 servings

Favorite recipe from **National Dairy Board**

HEARTY BEEF 'N' VEGETABLES

- **4 cups frozen potato rounds**
- **1 pound ground beef**
- **1 package (10 ounces) frozen chopped broccoli, thawed and drained**
- **1 can (2.8 ounces) FRENCH'S® French Fried Onions**
- **1 medium tomato, chopped (optional)**
- **1 can (10¾ ounces) condensed cream of celery soup**
- **⅓ cup milk**
- **1 cup (4 ounces) shredded Cheddar cheese**
- **¼ teaspoon garlic powder**
- **⅛ teaspoon freshly ground black pepper**

Preheat oven to 400°F.

Arrange frozen potatoes in bottom and up sides of 12 × 8-inch baking dish to form a shell. Bake, uncovered, at 400°F 10 minutes. In medium skillet, brown ground beef; drain well. Layer beef, broccoli, *½ can* French Fried Onions and tomato in potato shell. In small bowl, combine soup, milk, *½ cup* cheese and seasonings; pour evenly over beef mixture. Bake, covered, at 400°F 20 minutes or until heated through. Top with remaining cheese and onions; bake, uncovered, 1 to 3 minutes or until onions are golden brown.

Makes 4 to 6 servings

Overnight Cornbread Casserole

CHILI MEATLOAF & POTATO CASSEROLE

MEATLOAF

1½ **pounds lean ground beef**
¾ **cup finely chopped onion**
⅓ **cup saltine cracker crumbs**
1 **egg, slightly beaten**
3 **tablespoons milk**
1 **tablespoon chili powder**
¾ **teaspoon salt**

POTATO TOPPING

3 **cups prepared mashed potatoes**
1 **can (11 ounces) whole kernel corn with red and green peppers, drained**
¼ **cup thinly sliced green onions**
½ **to 1 cup shredded taco-seasoned cheese**

1. Preheat oven to 375°F. In large bowl combine ground beef, onion, crumbs, egg, milk, chili powder and salt; mix well. Gently press mixture on bottom of 9-inch square baking pan. Bake 20 to 25 minutes or until no longer pink in center and juices run clear. Carefully pour off juices.

2. Meanwhile, in medium bowl, combine mashed potatoes, corn with peppers and onions. Spread over meatloaf to edges of pan; sprinkle with cheese. Broil 3 to 4 inches from heat 3 to 5 minutes or until top is lightly browned.

Makes 6 servings

Favorite recipe from **National Live Stock & Meat Board**

OLD–FASHIONED BEEF POT PIE

1 **pound ground beef**
1 **can (11 ounces) condensed beef with vegetables and barley soup**
½ **cup water**
1 **package (10 ounces) frozen peas and carrots, thawed and drained**
½ **teaspoon seasoned salt**
⅛ **teaspoon garlic powder**
⅛ **teaspoon ground black pepper**
1 **cup (4 ounces) shredded Cheddar cheese**
1 **can (2.8 ounces) FRENCH'S® French Fried Onions**
1 **package (7.5 ounces) refrigerated biscuits**

Preheat oven to 350°F. In large skillet, brown ground beef in large chunks; drain. Stir in soup, water, vegetables and seasonings; bring to a boil. Reduce heat and simmer, uncovered, 5 minutes. Remove from heat; stir in ½ cup cheese and ½ can French Fried Onions.

Pour mixture into 12 × 8-inch baking dish. Cut each biscuit in half; place, cut side down, around edge of casserole. Bake, uncovered, 15 to 20 minutes or until biscuits are done. Top with remaining cheese and onions; bake, uncovered, 5 minutes or until onions are golden brown.

Makes 4 to 6 servings

Chili Meatloaf & Potato Casserole

MEATY MEALS

LAMB & GREEN CHILE STEW

1 pound boneless lean lamb, cubed
1 large onion, halved, sliced
6 cloves garlic, chopped or sliced
2 cans (15 ounces each) no-salt-added
   whole tomatoes, undrained
1 pound potatoes, peeled
3 cans (4 ounces each) diced mild green
   chilies
2 teaspoons dried rosemary leaves,
   crushed
1 teaspoon dried oregano leaves, crushed
1 pound zucchini
1 cup frozen whole kernel corn, thawed,
   drained
Pickled jalapeño peppers (optional)

Combine ½ cup water, lamb, onion and garlic in large saucepan. Bring to a simmer over medium-high heat. Cover; simmer 30 minutes or until onion is tender. Increase heat to high; uncover. Boil, stirring occasionally, until liquid evaporates and browns. Add tomatoes with liquid; stir. Reduce heat to medium-low. Cover; simmer 30 minutes.

Meanwhile, cut potatoes into 1½-inch pieces. Add potatoes, chilies, rosemary and oregano. Cover; simmer 20 to 30 minutes or until potatoes and lamb are tender.

Halve zucchini lengthwise and cut crosswise into ½- to ¼-inch pieces. Add zucchini and corn to stew. Cover; simmer 10 minutes or until zucchini is crisp-tender. Season with pepper. Garnish with jalapeños, if desired. *Makes 6 servings*

BEEF & BROCCOLI PEPPER STEAK

1 tablespoon margarine or butter
1 pound well-trimmed top round steak, cut
   into thin strips
1 package (6.8 ounces) RICE-A-RONI® Beef
   Flavor
2 cups broccoli flowerets
½ cup red or green bell pepper strips
1 small onion, thinly sliced

1. In large skillet, melt margarine over medium heat. Add meat; sauté just until browned.

2. Remove meat from skillet; set aside. Keep warm.

3. In same skillet, prepare Rice-A-Roni® Mix as package directs; simmer 10 minutes. Add meat and remaining ingredients; simmer an additional 10 minutes or until most of liquid is absorbed and vegetables are crisp-tender. *Makes 4 servings*

Lamb & Green Chile Stew

MEATY MEALS

COUNTDOWN CASSEROLE

1 jar (8 ounces) pasteurized process cheese spread
¾ cup milk
2 cups (12 ounces) cubed cooked roast beef
1 bag (16 ounces) frozen vegetable combination (broccoli, corn, red pepper), thawed and drained
4 cups frozen hash brown potatoes, thawed
1 can (2.8 ounces) FRENCH'S® French Fried Onions
½ teaspoon seasoned salt
¼ teaspoon freshly ground black pepper
½ cup (2 ounces) shredded Cheddar cheese

Preheat oven to 375°F. Spoon cheese spread into 12 × 8-inch baking dish; place in oven just until cheese melts, about 5 minutes. Using fork, stir milk into melted cheese until well blended. Stir in beef, vegetables, potatoes, *½ can* French Fried Onions and seasonings. Bake, covered, at 375°F 30 minutes or until heated through. Top with Cheddar cheese; sprinkle remaining onions down center. Bake, uncovered, 3 minutes or until onions are golden brown. *Makes 4 to 6 servings*

MICROWAVE DIRECTIONS: In 12 × 8-inch microwave-safe dish, combine cheese spread and milk. Cook, covered, on HIGH 3 minutes; stir. Add ingredients as directed. Cook, covered, 14 minutes or until heated through, stirring beef mixture halfway through cooking time. Top with Cheddar cheese and remaining onions as directed. Cook, uncovered, 1 minute or until cheese melts. Let stand 5 minutes.

PRIZE POTLUCK CASSEROLE

1 cup lentils, rinsed and drained
2 cups water
1 can (16 ounces) whole tomatoes, cut up, undrained
¼ cup minced onion
¼ cup chopped green pepper
1 teaspoon salt
½ teaspoon dry mustard
¼ teaspoon Worcestershire sauce
¼ teaspoon pepper
⅛ teaspoon thyme
1 pound Polish sausage, cut into 1½-inch-thick slices

Cook lentils in water until tender, about 30 minutes; drain if necessary. Preheat oven to 350°F. Combine lentils with tomatoes, onion, green pepper and seasonings. Turn into 13 × 9-inch casserole. Top with sausage. Cover casserole and bake 45 minutes. Uncover and bake 15 minutes longer. *Makes 6 servings*

Favorite recipe from USA Dry Pea & Lentil Council

Countdown Casserole

— *Fantastic* —

POTLUCK POULTRY

ORANGE GINGER CHICKEN & RICE

1 package (6.9 ounces) RICE-A-RONI® With
⅓ Less Salt Chicken Flavor
1 tablespoon margarine or butter
1 cup orange juice
¾ pound skinless, boneless chicken
breasts, cut into thin strips
2 cloves garlic, minced
¼ teaspoon ground ginger
Dash crushed red pepper flakes (optional)
1½ cups carrots, cut into short thin strips *or*
3 cups broccoli flowerets

1. In large skillet, sauté Rice-A-Roni® mix and margarine over medium heat, stirring frequently until vermicelli is golden brown.

2. Stir in 1½ cups water, orange juice, chicken, garlic, ginger, red pepper flakes and contents of seasoning packet; bring to a boil over high heat.

3. Cover; reduce heat. Simmer 10 minutes. Stir in carrots. Cover; continue to simmer 5 to 10 minutes or until liquid is absorbed and rice is tender.

Makes 4 servings

POTLUCK POULTRY

MICROWAVED GARLIC AND HERB CHICKEN

- 8 broiler-fryer chicken thighs (about 2 pounds)
- ½ cup olive oil
- 1 large tomato, chopped
- 1 rib celery, thinly sliced
- 2 tablespoons parsley flakes
- 6 cloves garlic, chopped
- 1 teaspoon salt
- ½ teaspoon ground black pepper
- ½ teaspoon dried oregano leaves
- ¼ teaspoon dried basil leaves
- ⅛ teaspoon ground nutmeg

MICROWAVE DIRECTIONS: In microwave-safe baking dish, mix together olive oil, tomato, celery, parsley, garlic, salt, pepper, oregano, basil and nutmeg. Microwave on HIGH (100% power) 3 minutes; stir. Add chicken; mix well. Cover; refrigerate 3 hours or overnight. Cover baking dish with waxed paper; microwave on HIGH 10 minutes. Turn chicken over; cover again with waxed paper and microwave on HIGH 10 minutes or until chicken is no longer pink in center. Let stand 5 minutes. To serve, remove garlic; discard. Spoon sauce over chicken.   *Makes 4 servings*

Favorite recipe from **National Broiler Council**

CHICKEN TETRAZZINI

- 8 ounces uncooked spaghetti, broken in half
- 3 tablespoons butter, divided
- ¼ cup all-purpose flour
- 1 teaspoon salt
- ½ teaspoon paprika
- ½ teaspoon celery salt
- ⅛ teaspoon pepper
- 2 cups milk
- 1 cup chicken broth
- 3 cups chopped cooked chicken
- 1 can (4 ounces) mushrooms, drained
- ¼ cup pimiento strips
- ¾ cup (3 ounces) grated Wisconsin Parmesan cheese, divided

In large saucepan, cook spaghetti according to package directions; drain. Return to same saucepan; add 1 tablespoon butter. Stir until melted. Set aside. In 3-quart saucepan, melt remaining 2 tablespoons butter over medium heat; stir in flour, salt, paprika, celery salt and pepper. Remove from heat; gradually stir in milk and chicken broth. Cook over medium heat, stirring constantly, until thickened. Add chicken, mushrooms, pimiento, spaghetti and ¼ cup cheese; heat thoroughly. Place chicken mixture on ovenproof platter or in shallow casserole; sprinkle remaining ½ cup cheese over top. Broil about 3 inches from heat until lightly browned.

Makes 6 to 8 servings

Favorite recipe from **Wisconsin Milk Marketing Board**

Microwaved Garlic and Herb Chicken

POTLUCK POULTRY

TURKEY–TORTILLA BAKE

9 (6-inch) corn tortillas
½ pound 93% fat free ground turkey
½ cup chopped onion
¾ cup mild or medium taco sauce
1 can (4 ounces) chopped green chilies, drained
½ cup frozen whole kernel corn, thawed
½ cup (2 ounces) shredded reduced fat Cheddar cheese

Preheat oven to 400°F. Place tortillas on large baking sheet, overlapping tortillas as little as possible. Bake 4 minutes; turn tortillas. Continue baking 2 minutes or until crisp. Cool completely on wire rack.

Heat medium nonstick skillet over medium heat until hot. Add turkey and onion. Cook and stir 5 minutes or until turkey is browned and onion is tender. Add taco sauce, chilies and corn. Reduce heat and simmer 5 minutes.

Break 3 tortillas and arrange on bottom of 1½-quart casserole. Spoon half the turkey mixture over the tortillas; sprinkle with half the cheese. Repeat layers. Bake 10 minutes or until cheese is melted and casserole is heated through. Break remaining tortillas and sprinkle over casserole. Garnish with reduced fat sour cream, if desired.

Makes 4 servings

SAVORY CHICKEN & BISCUITS

2 tablespoons olive or vegetable oil
1 pound boneless, skinless chicken breasts, cut into 1-inch pieces
1 medium onion, chopped
1 cup thinly sliced carrots
1 cup thinly sliced celery
1 envelope LIPTON® Recipe Secrets® Savory Herb with Garlic Soup Mix*
1 cup milk
1 package (10 ounces) refrigerated flaky buttermilk biscuits

Preheat oven to 375°F.

In 12-inch skillet, heat oil over medium-high heat. Add chicken; cook 5 minutes or until no longer pink. Stir in onion, carrots and celery; cook, stirring occasionally, 3 minutes. Stir in Savory Herb with Garlic Soup Mix blended with milk. Bring to a boil over medium-high heat, stirring occasionally; cook 1 minute. Turn into lightly greased 2-quart casserole; arrange biscuits on top of chicken mixture with edges touching. Bake 15 minutes or until biscuits are golden brown.

Makes 4 servings

*Also terrific with LIPTON® Recipe Secrets® Golden Onion or Golden Herb with Lemon Soup Mix.

POTLUCK POULTRY

SESAME CHICKEN AND VEGETABLE STIR–FRY

1 tablespoon Oriental sesame oil
1 pound chicken tenders, cut into 1-inch
    pieces
2 cups broccoli flowerettes
1 small red bell pepper, sliced
½ cup onion slices (about 1 small)
½ cup snow peas
1 can (8 ounces) water chestnuts, sliced
    and drained
2 cloves garlic, minced
1 teaspoon five-spice powder
1 cup defatted low sodium chicken broth
2 teaspoons cornstarch
2 tablespoons cold water
2 cups hot cooked rice

Heat sesame oil in wok or large nonstick skillet over medium heat until hot. Add chicken; stir-fry about 8 minutes or until chicken is no longer pink in center. Remove chicken from wok.

Add broccoli, bell pepper, onion, peas, water chestnuts and garlic to wok; stir-fry 5 to 8 minutes or until vegetables are crisp-tender. Sprinkle with five-spice powder; cook and stir 1 minute.

Return chicken to wok. Add chicken broth; heat to a boil. Combine cornstarch and water in small bowl; stir into broth mixture. Boil 1 to 2 minutes, stirring constantly. Serve over rice.

Makes 4 servings

CHICKEN TABBOULEH

1 cup bulgur or cracked wheat
3 cups hot water
1½ to 2 pounds boneless, skinless chicken
    breasts or thighs, cut into ½-inch cubes
1 teaspoon salt, divided
¼ teaspoon pepper, divided
½ cup plus 2 teaspoons olive or vegetable
    oil, divided
1 teaspoon butter or margarine
1 to 2 cups minced fresh parsley
¼ cup finely chopped onion
¼ cup plus 3 tablespoons fresh lemon juice
¼ teaspoon garlic powder
    Thin lemon slices for garnish

Soak bulgur in hot water in medium bowl 30 minutes.

Sprinkle chicken with $^1/_2$ teaspoon salt and $^1/_8$ teaspoon pepper. Heat 2 teaspoons oil and butter in large skillet over medium heat. Add chicken; cook, stirring frequently, until chicken is no longer pink in center, 3 to 5 minutes. Set aside.

Drain bulgur; transfer to large bowl. Add chicken, parsley, onion, remaining $^1/_2$ cup oil, lemon juice, remaining $^1/_2$ teaspoon salt, remaining $^1/_8$ teaspoon pepper and garlic powder. Toss well. Cover; refrigerate at least 1 hour. Garnish with lemon slices. *Makes 4 servings*

POTLUCK POULTRY

CHICKEN RAGOÛT

- 1 package (4.9 ounces) RICE-A-RONI® Chicken & Broccoli Flavor
- 3 tablespoons all-purpose flour
- ¾ teaspoon salt (optional)
- ½ teaspoon black pepper
- 1 pound skinless, boneless chicken breasts or thighs, cut into 1-inch pieces
- 2 tablespoons margarine or butter
- 2 cups sliced mushrooms
- 1 cup thinly sliced carrots
- 1 cup coarsely chopped onion
- 2 cloves garlic, minced
- ½ cup reduced-sodium or regular chicken broth
- ¼ cup dry white wine or additional chicken broth
- 1 teaspoon dried thyme leaves

1. Prepare Rice-A-Roni® Mix as package directs.

2. While Rice-A-Roni® is simmering, combine flour, salt and pepper. Coat chicken with flour mixture.

3. In second large skillet, melt margarine over medium heat. Add mushrooms, carrots, onion and garlic; cook 5 minutes, stirring occasionally. Add chicken; continue cooking 4 minutes, stirring occasionally. Add chicken broth, wine and thyme. Reduce heat to low.

4. Simmer 5 to 7 minutes or until chicken is cooked through and carrots are tender.

5. Serve rice topped with chicken mixture.

Makes 4 servings

ONE–DISH CHICKEN 'N' RICE

- 1 cup uncooked regular or converted rice
- 1 medium red bell pepper, sliced
- 1 medium onion, cut into wedges
- 1 envelope LIPTON® Recipe Secrets® Golden Herb with Lemon or Savory Herb with Garlic Soup Mix
- 1½ cups water
- 1 cup orange juice
- ½ teaspoon salt
- 4 boneless skinless chicken breast halves (about 1 pound)

Preheat oven to 350°F.

In 13 × 9-inch casserole, combine uncooked rice, red pepper and onion. Add Golden Herb with Lemon Soup Mix blended with water, orange juice and salt. Arrange chicken on rice, spooning some liquid over chicken. Cover and bake 45 minutes or until chicken is no longer pink in center and rice is done. Garnish with orange slices and fresh chopped parsley. *Makes 4 servings*

Chicken Ragoût

POTLUCK POULTRY

CHICKEN AND VEGGIE LASAGNA

Tomato-Herb Sauce (recipe follows)
Nonstick olive oil cooking spray
1½ **cups thinly sliced zucchini**
1 **cup thinly sliced carrots**
3 **cups torn fresh spinach leaves**
½ **teaspoon salt**
1 **package (15 ounces) fat free ricotta**
   cheese
½ **cup grated Parmesan cheese**
9 **lasagna noodles, cooked and drained**
2 **cups (8 ounces) reduced fat shredded**
   mozzarella cheese, divided

Prepare Tomato-Herb Sauce. Preheat oven to 350°F. Spray large nonstick skillet with cooking spray; heat over medium heat until hot. Add zucchini and carrots; cook and stir about 5 minutes or until almost tender. Remove from heat; stir in spinach and salt.

Combine ricotta and Parmesan cheese in small bowl. Spread 1⅔ cups Tomato-Herb Sauce on bottom of 13 × 9-inch baking pan. Top with 3 noodles. Spoon half the ricotta cheese mixture over noodles; spread lightly with spatula. Spoon half the zucchini mixture over ricotta cheese mixture; sprinkle with 1 cup mozzarella cheese. Repeat layers; place remaining 3 noodles on top.

Spread remaining Tomato-Herb Sauce over noodles. Cover with aluminum foil; bake 1 hour or until sauce is bubbly. Let stand 5 to 10 minutes; cut into rectangles. Garnish as desired.

Makes 12 servings

Tomato-Herb Sauce

Nonstick olive oil cooking spray
1½ **cups chopped onions (about 2 medium)**
4 **cloves garlic, minced**
1 **tablespoon dried basil leaves**
1 **teaspoon dried oregano leaves**
½ **teaspoon dried tarragon leaves**
¼ **teaspoon dried thyme leaves**
2½ **pounds ripe tomatoes, peeled and cut into**
   wedges
1 **pound ground chicken, cooked, crumbled**
   and drained
¾ **cup water**
¼ **cup no-salt-added tomato paste**
½ **teaspoon salt**
½ **teaspoon pepper**

Spray large nonstick skillet with cooking spray; heat over medium heat until hot. Add onions, garlic, basil, oregano, tarragon and thyme; cook and stir about 5 minutes or until onions are tender.

Add tomatoes, chicken, water and tomato paste; heat to a boil. Reduce heat to low and simmer, uncovered, about 20 minutes or until sauce is reduced to 5 cups. Stir in salt and pepper.

Makes 5 cups

Chicken and Veggie Lasagna

POTLUCK POULTRY

CHICKEN BOURGUIGNONNE

**4 pounds skinless chicken thighs and
    breasts
Flour
Nonstick cooking spray
2 cups defatted low sodium chicken broth
2 cups dry white wine or defatted low
    sodium chicken broth
1 pound whole baby carrots
¼ cup tomato paste
4 cloves garlic, minced
½ teaspoon dried thyme leaves
2 bay leaves
¼ teaspoon salt
¼ teaspoon pepper
8 ounces fresh or thawed frozen pearl
    onions
8 ounces whole medium mushrooms
2 cups hot cooked white rice
2 cups hot cooked wild rice
¼ cup minced fresh parsley**

Preheat oven to 325°F. Coat chicken very lightly
with flour. Generously spray nonstick ovenproof
Dutch oven or large nonstick ovenproof skillet
with cooking spray; heat over medium heat until
hot. Cook chicken 10 to 15 minutes or until
browned on all sides. Drain fat from Dutch oven.

Add chicken broth, wine, carrots, tomato paste,
garlic, thyme, bay leaves, salt and pepper to Dutch
oven; heat to a boil. Cover; transfer to oven. Bake
1 hour. Add onions and mushrooms. Uncover;
bake about 35 minutes or until vegetables are

tender and chicken is no longer pink in center and
juices run clear. Remove bay leaves. Combine
white and wild rice; serve with chicken. Sprinkle
with parsley.   *Makes 8 servings*

CHICKEN & WILD RICE

**6 cups cooked wild rice (1½ cups
    uncooked)
1 can (10¾ ounces) cream of chicken soup
1 can (10¾ ounces) cream of celery soup
1 can (about 14 ounces) chicken broth
1 can (4 ounces) mushrooms, drained
3 cups diced cooked chicken
¼ cup chopped green bell pepper
¼ cup chopped red bell pepper
¼ teaspoon garlic powder
½ cup slivered almonds**

Preheat oven to 350°F. Grease 13 × 9-inch
casserole.

Mix rice, soups, broth, mushrooms, chicken, bell
peppers and garlic powder in large bowl. Spread in
prepared dish. Sprinkle with almonds. Bake,
covered, 45 minutes. Uncover and continue baking
15 minutes or until heated through.
                     Makes 10 to 12 servings

*Favorite recipe from **Minnesota Cultivated Wild Rice Council***

Chicken Bourguignonne

POTLUCK POULTRY

CHICKEN FIESTA

2½ to 3 pounds chicken pieces
   Salt
   Pepper
   Paprika
 2 tablespoons butter or margarine
 ¼ pound pork sausage
 ¾ cup sliced celery
 ¾ cup sliced green onions with tops
 3 cups cooked rice
 1 can (12 ounces) whole kernel corn with
   peppers, drained
 2 teaspoons lemon juice

Preheat oven to 350°F.

Season chicken with salt, pepper and paprika. In
large skillet, melt butter. Add chicken to skillet;
brown well. Drain chicken on paper towels; set
aside. Cook sausage, celery and onions in same
skillet over medium-high heat, stirring frequently
until vegetables are crisp-tender. Add rice, corn
and lemon juice; mix well. Pour into shallow
baking dish. Arrange chicken on top of rice
mixture, pressing chicken slightly into rice
mixture. Cover with foil. Bake 30 to 40 minutes or
until chicken is no longer pink in center.

Makes 6 servings

Favorite recipe from **USA Rice Council**

CHICKEN VEGETABLE SKILLET

 8 broiler-fryer chicken thighs, skinned, fat
   trimmed
 ¾ teaspoon salt, divided
 1 tablespoon vegetable oil
 3 medium red-skinned potatoes, cut into
   ¼-inch slices
 1 medium onion, sliced
 ½ pound fresh mushrooms, sliced
 1 large tomato, coarsely chopped
 ¼ cup chicken broth
 ¼ cup dry white wine
 ½ teaspoon oregano
 ¼ teaspoon pepper
 1 tablespoon chopped fresh parsley

Sprinkle chicken with ¼ teaspoon salt. Heat oil in
large nonstick saucepan over medium-high heat.
Add chicken and cook, turning once, about 8
minutes or until browned on both sides. Remove
chicken; set aside. In same pan, layer potatoes,
onion, chicken, mushrooms and tomato.

In 1-cup measure, mix together broth and wine;
pour over chicken and vegetables. Sprinkle
oregano, remaining ½ teaspoon salt and pepper
over chicken. Heat to boiling; cover. Reduce heat
to medium-low; cook about 20 minutes or until
chicken and vegetables are fork-tender. Sprinkle
with fresh parsley before serving.

Makes 4 servings

Chicken Fiesta

POTLUCK POULTRY

CORN AND CHICKEN CASSEROLE

2 whole chickens (2 to 3 pounds each), each cut into 10 pieces
3 tablespoons Chef Paul Prudhomme's POULTRY MAGIC®, divided
⅓ cup vegetable oil
8 cups fresh corn, cut off cob (about twelve 8-inch ears)
3½ cups finely chopped onions
1½ cups finely chopped green bell peppers
1 pound tomatoes, peeled, chopped
3½ cups chicken stock
2 cups uncooked rice

Remove excess fat from chicken; season with 2 tablespoons POULTRY MAGIC® and place in plastic bag. Seal and refrigerate overnight.

Heat oil in an 8-quart roasting pan over high heat until oil just starts to smoke, about 6 minutes. Add 10 pieces of chicken (skin side down) and brown, cooking 5 minutes on each side. Remove chicken; brown remaining chicken 5 minutes on each side. Remove and keep warm.

Add half the corn to hot oil; stir well. Cook, without stirring, about 6 minutes. Stir in 1½ teaspoons POULTRY MAGIC®. Cook, without stirring, about 7 minutes. Stir in onions, bell peppers, and remaining 1½ teaspoons POULTRY MAGIC®. Cover with tight-fitting lid and cook 5 minutes. Add remaining corn and tomatoes; mix

well. Cover and cook 10 minutes. Transfer corn mixture to another pan and keep warm. Preheat oven to 400°F.

Add stock and rice to roasting pan. Bring to a boil, stirring occasionally. Layer chicken pieces on top of rice. Cover chicken layer with corn mixture. Cover and bake 25 minutes.

Remove casserole from oven. Let stand 10 minutes. *Makes 8 servings*

LAYERED CHICKEN & VEGETABLE BAKE

1 package RITZ® Stuffing Mix
¾ cup water
1 pound chicken tenders
1 large tomato, sliced ¼ inch thick
1 medium zucchini, sliced ¼ inch thick
1 cup shredded mozzarella cheese

In small bowl, toss stuffing crumbs, seasoning packet and water. Place half of mixture in lightly greased 9-inch square baking pan. Place chicken on top; cover with remaining stuffing mixture. Layer tomato and zucchini on top; cover with cheese.

Bake at 375°F 30 to 35 minutes or until top is lightly browned. Cut into squares.

Makes 4 servings

POTLUCK POULTRY

BUFFET CHICKEN MEDLEY

4 boneless, skinless chicken breasts, quartered (about 2½ pounds)
2 tablespoons butter or margarine
1 large onion, cut into ¼-inch pieces
1 jar (6 ounces) marinated artichoke hearts, drained and sliced (reserve marinade)
4 tomatoes, cut into wedges
1 teaspoon salt, divided
½ teaspoon pepper, divided
1 avocado, halved, peeled, pitted and cut into ½-inch wedges
1 cup (4 ounces) crumbled feta cheese

In 10-inch skillet, melt butter over medium-high heat. Add chicken pieces; cook, turning, about 5 minutes or until lightly browned. Remove chicken to warm dish.

Add onion to pan juices; cook over medium heat 3 minutes, stirring frequently. Add artichokes, reserved marinade and tomatoes; cook about 2 minutes. Remove from heat. In 2-quart baking dish, place half of chicken; sprinkle with ¹/₂ teaspoon salt and ¹/₄ teaspoon pepper. Spoon half of artichoke mixture over chicken; add half of avocado and half of cheese. Top with remaining chicken; repeat layers. Bake at 350°F about 25 minutes or until chicken is no longer pink in center.

Makes 8 servings

Favorite recipe from **National Broiler Council**

"WILDLY" DELICIOUS CASSEROLE

1 package (14 ounces) ground chicken
1 package (14 ounces) frozen broccoli with red peppers
1½ cups cooked wild rice
1 can (10¾ ounces) condensed cream of chicken soup
½ cup mayonnaise
½ cup plain yogurt
1 teaspoon lemon juice
½ teaspoon curry powder
¼ cup dry bread crumbs
3 to 4 slices process American cheese, cut in half diagonally

Preheat oven to 375°F. Grease 8-inch square casserole; set aside. In large skillet, cook chicken until no longer pink. Drain; set aside. Cook broccoli and peppers according to package directions; set aside. In large bowl, combine rice, soup, mayonnaise, yogurt, lemon juice and curry. Stir in chicken and broccoli and peppers. Pour into prepared casserole; sprinkle with bread crumbs. Bake 45 to 55 minutes. During last 5 minutes of baking, arrange cheese slices on top of casserole. Remove from oven; let stand 5 minutes.

Makes 6 to 8 servings

Favorite recipe from **Minnesota Cultivated Wild Rice Council**

POTLUCK POULTRY

CELERY, POTATO AND CHICKEN SKILLET STEW

1 pound red-skinned potatoes, cut into
    ¾-inch chunks
2 cups sliced celery, divided
½ cup chopped celery leaves, divided
1 tablespoon vegetable oil
12 ounces boneless, skinless chicken
    breasts, cut into 1-inch pieces
1 cup chopped red bell pepper
3 tablespoons tomato paste
½ teaspoon dried rosemary leaves, crushed
½ teaspoon sugar
¼ teaspoon ground black pepper
    Salt

Bring 1 quart water to a boil in medium saucepan over high heat. Add potatoes, 1 cup celery and ¼ cup celery leaves. Reduce heat to medium; simmer, covered, 7 to 8 minutes or until potatoes are tender. Drain, reserving cooking liquid and vegetables separately. Heat oil in large nonstick skillet over medium-high heat. Add chicken, bell pepper and remaining 1 cup celery. Cook, stirring constantly, 6 to 7 minutes or until chicken is no longer pink. Stir in tomato paste, rosemary, sugar, black pepper and 2 cups reserved potato liquid. Bring to a boil; cook until sauce thickens, about 4 minutes. Add reserved potatoes and celery. Season to taste with salt. Sprinkle with remaining ¼ cup celery leaves. *Makes 4 servings*

Favorite recipe from **American Celery Council**

TURKEY WILD RICE SUPREME

2 pounds ground turkey
1 can (8 ounces) mushrooms, drained
1 cup chopped onions
½ cup chopped celery
½ cup shredded carrots
½ cup butter
2 cups sour cream
¼ cup soy sauce
1 teaspoon salt
¼ teaspoon pepper
6 cups cooked wild rice (1½ cups
    uncooked)
½ cup slivered almonds
    Parsley sprigs, optional

Preheat oven to 350°F. Grease 3-quart casserole. Set aside.

Brown turkey in large skillet; set aside. Cook and stir mushrooms, onions, celery and carrots in butter 5 to 10 minutes. In large bowl combine sour cream, soy sauce, salt and pepper. Add wild rice, turkey, mushroom mixture and almonds. Toss lightly. Place mixture in prepared casserole. Bake 1 hour or until lightly browned, stirring several times during baking and adding more water, if needed. Season to taste. Garnish with parsley.
Makes 10 to 12 servings

Favorite recipe from **Minnesota Cultivated Wild Rice Council**

Celery, Potato and Chicken Skillet Stew

— *Spectacular* —

DEEP SEA DINNERS

HOMESTYLE TUNA POT PIE

**1 package (15 ounces) refrigerated pie
  crusts
1 can (12 ounces) STARKIST® Solid White
  or Chunk Light Tuna, drained and
  chunked
1 package (10 ounces) frozen peas and
  carrots, thawed and drained
½ cup chopped onion
1 can (10¾ ounces) cream of potato or
  cream of mushroom soup
⅓ cup milk
½ teaspoon poultry seasoning or dried
  thyme
Salt and pepper to taste**

Line 9-inch pie pan with one crust; set aside. Reserve second crust. In medium bowl, combine remaining ingredients; mix well. Pour tuna mixture into pie shell; top with second crust. Crimp edges to seal. Cut slits in top crust to vent. Bake in 375°F oven 45 to 50 minutes or until golden brown. *Makes 6 servings*

BAKED ROCKFISH VERACRUZ

1 teaspoon olive oil
½ small onion, chopped
4 cloves garlic, minced
8 to 10 ounces ripe tomatoes, cored and chopped *or* 2 cans (15 ounces each) no-salt-added whole tomatoes, drained, chopped
½ green bell pepper, chopped
½ to 1 jalapeño pepper, seeded, minced (optional)
1 teaspoon dried oregano leaves, crushed
½ teaspoon ground cumin
¼ cup small pimiento-stuffed green olives
2 teaspoons drained capers (optional)
1 pound skinless fillets rockfish, snapper, halibut or cod

Preheat oven to 375°F. Heat large nonstick skillet over medium-high heat. Add oil, onion and garlic. Cook and stir 3 minutes or until onion is tender. Add tomatoes, bell pepper, jalapeño, oregano and cumin. Cook over high heat, stirring occasionally, 2 to 3 minutes more. Stir in olives and capers, if desired; set aside.

Spray 11 × 7-inch baking pan with nonstick cooking spray. Place fish in single layer in pan, folding thin tail sections under to make fish evenly thick. Pour tomato mixture over fish. Cover with foil; bake 10 minutes or until fish is opaque and flakes easily when tested with fork. Serve with rice and garnish with fresh herbs, if desired.

Makes 4 servings

SEAFOOD GUMBO

½ cup sliced celery
½ cup chopped onion
½ cup chopped green bell pepper
1 clove garlic, minced
1 tablespoon vegetable oil
1 can (13¾ ounces) chicken broth
1 can (14 to 16 ounces) whole tomatoes, cut into bite-size pieces
2 cups fresh or frozen sliced okra
¾ cup HEINZ® Chili Sauce
½ teaspoon salt
¼ teaspoon black pepper
¼ teaspoon dried thyme leaves
1 bay leaf
    Dash hot pepper sauce
1 pound white fish fillets, cut into 1-inch pieces
    Hot cooked rice (about 1⅓ cups)

In 3-quart saucepan, sauté celery, onion, bell pepper and garlic in oil until crisp-tender. Add broth, tomatoes, okra, chili sauce, salt, black pepper, thyme, bay leaf and hot pepper sauce. Simmer, covered, 20 minutes. Add fish; simmer, covered, 15 to 20 minutes. Remove bay leaf. Place about ⅓ cup rice in each serving bowl; top with gumbo. *Makes 4 servings (about 6 cups)*

Baked Rockfish Veracruz

BISCUIT-TOPPED TUNA BAKE

- 2 tablespoons vegetable oil
- ½ cup chopped onion
- ½ cup chopped celery
- 1 can (12 ounces) STARKIST® Solid White or Chunk Light Tuna, drained and chunked
- 1 can (10¾ ounces) condensed cream of potato soup
- 1 package (10 ounces) frozen peas and carrots, thawed
- ¾ cup milk
- ¼ teaspoon ground black pepper
- ¼ teaspoon garlic powder
- 1 can (7½ ounces) refrigerator flaky biscuits

In large skillet, heat oil over medium-high heat; sauté onion and celery until onion is soft. Add remaining ingredients except biscuits; heat thoroughly. Transfer mixture to 1½-quart casserole. Arrange biscuits around top edge of dish; bake in 400°F oven 10 to 15 minutes or until biscuits are golden brown.

Makes 4 to 6 servings

Prep and Cook Time: 25 minutes

SHRIMP CASSEROLE

- ¾ pound raw medium shrimp, peeled, deveined
- ⅓ cup chopped celery
- ¼ cup chopped green bell pepper
- ¼ cup chopped onion
- 3 tablespoons margarine or butter
- 1 can (10¾ ounces) condensed cream of celery or cream of mushroom soup
- ⅓ cup sliced water chestnuts
- 1 hard-boiled egg, chopped
- 1 tablespoon lemon juice
- ½ cup dry stuffing mix
- ¼ teaspoon salt
- ¼ cup (1 ounce) shredded Cheddar cheese

Cut any large shrimp in half. In 1½-quart shallow casserole, combine shrimp, celery, bell pepper, onion and margarine. Cover and cook on HIGH (100% power) 4 minutes, stirring after 2 minutes. Stir in soup, water chestnuts, egg, lemon juice, stuffing mix and salt. Cover and cook on HIGH 4 minutes, rotating dish once. Sprinkle casserole with cheese; cook, uncovered, on HIGH 1 minute.

Makes 4 servings

Favorite recipe from Florida Department of Agriculture and Consumer Services Bureau of Seafood and Aquaculture

Biscuit-Topped Tuna Bake

SALMON LINGUINI SUPPER

8 ounces linguini, cooked in unsalted water and drained
1 package (10 ounces) frozen peas
1 cup milk
1 can (10¾ ounces) condensed cream of celery soup
¼ cup (1 ounce) grated Parmesan cheese
⅛ teaspoon tarragon, crumbled (optional)
1 can (15½ ounces) salmon, drained and flaked
1 egg, slightly beaten
¼ teaspoon salt
¼ teaspoon ground black pepper
1 can (2.8 ounces) FRENCH'S® French Fried Onions, divided

Preheat oven to 375°F. Place cooked pasta in saucepan; stir in peas, milk, soup, cheese and tarragon. Spoon into 12 × 8-inch baking dish. In medium bowl, using fork, combine salmon, egg, salt, pepper and *½ can* French Fried Onions. Shape salmon mixture into 4 oval patties. Place patties on pasta mixture. Bake, covered, at 375°F 40 minutes or until patties are done. Top patties with remaining onions; bake, uncovered, 3 minutes or until onions are golden brown.

Makes 4 servings

MICROWAVE DIRECTIONS: Prepare pasta mixture as above, except increase milk to 1¼ cups; spoon into 12 × 8-inch microwavable dish. Cook, covered, at HIGH (100% power) 3 minutes; stir. Prepare salmon patties as above, except use 2 eggs.

Place patties on pasta mixture. Cook, covered, at HIGH (100% power) 10 to 12 minutes or until patties are done. Rotate dish halfway through cooking time. Top patties with remaining onions; cook, uncovered, at HIGH (100% power) 1 minute. Let stand 5 minutes.

CRAB AND BROWN RICE CASSEROLE

1 pound fresh or thawed frozen blue crabmeat
3 eggs, slightly beaten
1 cup mayonnaise
1 cup cooked brown rice
¾ cup evaporated milk
¾ cup (3 ounces) shredded Cheddar cheese
¼ teaspoon hot pepper sauce

Preheat oven to 350°F. Grease 1½-quart casserole; set aside. Remove any pieces of cartilage from crabmeat. Set aside.

Combine eggs, mayonnaise, brown rice, milk, cheese and hot pepper sauce in large bowl. Stir in crabmeat. Bake 30 to 35 minutes or until knife inserted 1 inch from center comes out clean.

Makes 6 servings

Favorite recipe from Florida Department of Agriculture and Consumer Services Bureau of Seafood and Aquaculture

Salmon Linguini Supper

THAI-STYLE TUNA FRIED RICE

4 to 5 tablespoons vegetable oil, divided
2 eggs, lightly beaten
⅔ cup uncooked, peeled medium shrimp, chopped into ¾-inch pieces
3 cloves garlic
1 to 2 tablespoons minced fresh serrano chiles
4 to 6 cups cooked rice, chilled overnight
1 tablespoon sugar
1 tablespoon nam pla (fish sauce) (optional)
1 tablespoon soy sauce
1 can (6 ounces) STARKIST® Solid White or Chunk Light Tuna, drained and chunked
½ cup chopped dry-roasted peanuts
¼ cup chopped fresh basil
2 tablespoons chopped fresh cilantro
Lime wedges, for garnish

In wok, heat 1 tablespoon oil over medium-high heat; add eggs and cook, stirring, until partially cooked but still runny. Return eggs to bowl. Wipe out wok with paper towels. Add 2 tablespoons oil to wok; heat.

Add shrimp, garlic and chiles. Stir-fry until shrimp turn pink, about 3 minutes. Remove shrimp mixture; set aside. Add 1 or 2 tablespoons oil to wok; stir-fry rice, sugar, nam pla, if desired, and soy sauce until rice is heated through. Add tuna and peanuts; heat.

Return shrimp mixture and eggs to pan, chopping eggs into pieces with stir-fry spatula. Add basil and cilantro; toss gently to mix. Serve with lime wedges for garnish; squeeze juice on fried rice, if desired. *Makes 4 to 6 servings*

Prep and Cook Time: 15 minutes

SURFER'S SEAFOOD CASSEROLE

½ pound fresh crabmeat
½ pound cooked, peeled, deveined shrimp
1⅓ cups chopped celery
½ cup chopped onion
½ cup chopped green bell pepper
½ teaspoon salt
1 cup mayonnaise
1 teaspoon Worcestershire sauce
1 cup crushed potato chips
Paprika

Preheat oven to 350°F. Grease 1½-quart casserole; set aside.

Mix crabmeat, shrimp, celery, onion, bell pepper, salt, mayonnaise and Worcestershire in large bowl. Pour crab mixture into prepared casserole. Top with crushed potato chips and paprika. Bake 30 to 40 minutes or until knife inserted in center comes out clean. *Makes 6 servings*

*Favorite recipe from **Florida Department of Agriculture and Consumer Services Bureau of Seafood and Aquaculture***

Thai-Style Tuna Fried Rice

DEEP SEA DINNERS

LOUISIANA SHRIMP CREOLE PIE

**9-inch Classic Crisco® Double Crust
(page 11)**
SHRIMP FILLING
½ cup butter or margarine
¼ cup all-purpose flour
1 cup chopped onion
½ cup thinly sliced green onion tops
⅓ cup chopped green bell pepper
3 tablespoons chopped celery
3 tablespoons finely minced fresh parsley
2 teaspoons finely minced garlic
1 teaspoon salt
¾ teaspoon black pepper
¼ cup whipping cream
3 tablespoons brandy (optional)
2 pounds shelled and deveined small shrimp (crawfish tail meat can be substituted)

1. For crust, heat oven to 350°F. Follow steps 4 and 5 on page 11.

2. Divide dough in half. Roll and press bottom crust into 9-inch deep dish pie plate. Trim edge even with pie plate. *Do not bake.*

3. For filling, melt butter in 10-inch skillet over medium heat. Add flour; cook, stirring constantly, 3 minutes or until light golden brown. Add chopped onion, sliced green onions, green bell pepper, celery, parsley and garlic. Cook, stirring constantly, until vegetables are very soft. Add salt,

black pepper, whipping cream and brandy, if used. Mix gently, reduce heat to low, and cook an additional 3 minutes. Add shrimp and cook until tender. Remove from heat and allow filling to cool slightly.

4. Spoon filling into unbaked 9-inch pie shell. Roll top crust same as bottom. Lift top crust onto filled pie. Fold top edge under bottom crust; flute or make rope edge. Cut slits or design in top crust to allow steam to escape.

5. Bake pie 25 to 30 minutes or until top is golden.
Makes 8 servings

FISH BROCCOLI CASSEROLE

1 package (10 ounces) frozen broccoli spears, thawed, drained
1 cup cooked, flaked whitefish
1 can (10¾ ounces) condensed cream of mushroom soup
½ cup milk
¼ teaspoon salt
⅛ teaspoon freshly ground black pepper
½ cup crushed potato chips

Preheat oven to 425°F. Grease 1½-quart casserole. Place broccoli in single layer in casserole. Combine fish, soup, milk, salt and pepper in large bowl.

Spread fish mixture over broccoli. Sprinkle with potato chips. Bake 12 to 15 minutes or until golden brown. *Makes 4 servings*

Favorite recipe from Florida Department of Agriculture and Consumer Services Bureau of Seafood and Aquaculture

TUNA POT PIE

**9-inch Classic Crisco® Single Crust
(page 10)**
FILLING
  **1 tablespoon CRISCO® all-vegetable
    shortening**
  ¼ cup minced onion
  3 tablespoons all-purpose flour
  ¼ teaspoon dill weed
  ¼ teaspoon marjoram
  ¼ teaspoon salt
  1½ cups skim milk
  **1 can (12½ to 13 ounces) solid white tuna in
    water, drained**
  **1 (16-ounce) package frozen vegetable
    blend containing cauliflower, carrots,
    broccoli, green beans and lima beans**
  ½ cup frozen peas
GLAZE
  1 egg white, lightly beaten
  ⅛ teaspoon dill weed

1. For crust, prepare dough following steps 6 and 7 on page 10. See step 3 on this page for rolling directions.

2. For filling, in 3-quart saucepan over medium heat, melt shortening. Add onion; cook, stirring often, until tender. Combine flour, dill weed, marjoram and salt; stir into onion mixture. Cook, stirring often, 1 minute. Stir in milk gradually; cook and stir until mixture thickens. Remove from heat. Break up tuna into bite-size pieces with fork; stir tuna, frozen vegetable blend and peas into mixture in saucepan.

3. Between lightly floured sheets of waxed paper, roll dough "pancake" into rectangle 1 inch larger than inverted 12 × 7½ × 1½-inch baking dish. Peel off top sheet.

4. Preheat oven to 400°F. Pour filling into baking dish. Moisten edge of dish with water. Flip crust onto filled dish. Remove waxed paper. Fold edge of pastry under. Flute. Cut slits or design in crust to allow steam to escape.

5. For glaze, brush egg white over crust. Sprinkle with dill weed. Bake pie 30 to 35 minutes or until crust is golden brown.   *Makes 8 servings*

CLAM BAKE PIE

3 slices bacon
¼ cup chopped onion
¼ cup unsifted flour
1 (15-ounce) can SNOW'S® or DOXSEE®
  Condensed New England Clam
  Chowder
1 (6½-ounce) can SNOW'S® or DOXSEE®
  Chopped or Minced Clams, drained,
  reserving ¼ cup liquid
1 cup whole kernel corn
½ cup BORDEN® or MEADOW GOLD® Half-
  and-Half
2 tablespoons chopped fresh parsley *or*
  1 tablespoon dried parsley flakes
Pastry for 2-crust 9-inch pie

Place rack in lowest position in oven; preheat oven
to 425°F. In medium skillet, cook bacon until
crisp; remove and crumble bacon, reserving
2 tablespoons bacon drippings in skillet. Add
onion; cook until tender. Stir in flour until smooth.
Add chowder, reserved clam liquid, corn and half-
and-half; cook and stir until thickened. Stir in
clams, bacon and parsley. Turn into pastry-lined
9-inch pie plate. Cover with top crust; cut slits
near center. Seal and flute. Bake 30 minutes or
until golden. Let stand 20 minutes before serving.
Garnish as desired. Refrigerate leftovers.

Makes 1 (9-inch) pie

FISH & CHOWDER PIE

½ pound white fish fillets, fresh or frozen,
  thawed, cut into small pieces
1 (15-ounce) can SNOW'S® or DOXSEE®
  Condensed New England Clam
  Chowder
2 (6½-ounce) cans SNOW'S® or DOXSEE®
  Chopped or Minced Clams, drained,
  reserving ¼ cup liquid
⅓ cup BORDEN® or MEADOW GOLD® Half-
  and-Half or Milk
1 (10-ounce) package frozen peas and
  carrots, thawed
¼ cup unsifted flour
½ teaspoon dried thyme leaves, crumbled
⅛ to ¼ teaspoon pepper
Pastry for 1-crust 10-inch pie

Preheat oven to 400°F. In 1½-quart baking dish,
combine all ingredients except pastry. Top with
pastry; cut slits near center. Seal and flute. Bake 1
hour or until golden brown. Let stand 10 minutes
before serving. Refrigerate leftovers.

Makes 6 to 8 servings

*Top to bottom: Fish and Chowder
Pie; Clam Bake Pie*

DEEP SEA DINNERS

LEMON–GARLIC SHRIMP

1 package (6.2 ounces) RICE-A-RONI® With ⅓ Less Salt Broccoli Au Gratin
1 tablespoon margarine or butter
1 pound raw medium shrimp, shelled, deveined or large scallops, halved
1 medium red or green bell pepper, cut into short thin strips
2 cloves garlic, minced
½ teaspoon Italian seasoning
½ cup reduced-sodium or regular chicken broth
1 tablespoon lemon juice
1 tablespoon cornstarch
3 medium green onions, cut into ½-inch pieces
1 teaspoon grated lemon peel

1. Prepare Rice-A-Roni Mix as package directs.

2. While Rice-A-Roni is simmering, heat margarine in second large skillet or wok over medium-high heat. Add shrimp, red pepper, garlic and Italian seasoning. Stir-fry 3 to 4 minutes or until seafood is opaque.

3. Combine chicken broth, lemon juice and cornstarch, mixing until smooth. Add broth mixture and onions to skillet. Stir-fry 2 to 3 minutes or until sauce thickens.

4. Stir ½ teaspoon lemon peel into rice. Serve rice topped with shrimp mixture; sprinkle with remaining ½ teaspoon lemon peel.

Makes 4 servings

EASY THREE CHEESE TUNA SOUFFLÉ

4 cups large garlic and herb or ranch-flavored croutons
2½ cups milk
4 large eggs
1 can (10¾ ounces) cream of celery soup
3 cups shredded cheese (a combination of Cheddar, Monterey Jack and Swiss)
1 can (12 ounces) STARKIST® Solid White or Chunk Light Tuna, drained and flaked
1 tablespoon butter or margarine
½ cup chopped celery
½ cup finely chopped onion
¼ pound mushrooms, sliced

In bottom of lightly greased 13 × 9-inch baking dish, arrange croutons. In medium bowl, beat together milk, eggs and soup; stir in cheeses and tuna. In small skillet, melt butter over medium heat. Add celery, onion and mushrooms; sauté until onion is soft.

Spoon sautéed vegetables over croutons; pour egg-tuna mixture over top. Cover; refrigerate overnight. Remove from refrigerator 1 hour before baking; bake in 325°F oven 45 to 50 minutes or until hot and bubbly. *Makes 8 servings*

Prep and Cook Time: 60 minutes

Lemon–Garlic Shrimp

CRAB AND CORN ENCHILADA CASSEROLE

Spicy Tomato Sauce (recipe follows), divided
10 to 12 ounces fresh crabmeat or flaked or chopped imitation crabmeat
1 package (10 ounces) frozen whole kernel corn, thawed, drained
1½ cups (6 ounces) shredded reduced fat Monterey Jack cheese, divided
1 can (4 ounces) diced mild green chilies
12 (6-inch) corn tortillas
1 lime, cut into 6 wedges
Low fat sour cream (optional)

Preheat oven to 350°F. Combine 2 cups Spicy Tomato Sauce, crabmeat, corn, 1 cup cheese and chilies in medium bowl.

Cut each tortilla into 4 wedges. Place one-third of tortilla wedges in bottom of shallow 3- to 4-quart casserole, overlapping to make solid layer. Spread half of crab mixture on top. Repeat with another layer of tortilla wedges, remaining crab mixture and remaining tortillas. Spread remaining 1 cup Spicy Tomato Sauce over top; cover.

Bake 30 to 40 minutes or until heated through. Sprinkle with remaining ½ cup cheese and bake uncovered 5 minutes or until cheese melts. Squeeze lime over individual servings. Serve with low fat sour cream, if desired.   *Makes 6 servings*

Spicy Tomato Sauce
2 cans (15 ounces each) no-salt-added stewed tomatoes, undrained *or* 6 medium tomatoes
2 teaspoons olive oil
1 medium onion, chopped
1 tablespoon minced garlic
2 tablespoons chili powder
2 teaspoons ground cumin
2 teaspoons dried oregano leaves, crushed
1 teaspoon ground cinnamon
¼ teaspoon crushed red pepper
¼ teaspoon ground cloves

Combine tomatoes with liquid in food processor or blender; process until finely chopped. Set aside.

Heat oil over medium-high heat in large saucepan or Dutch oven. Add onion and garlic. Cook and stir 5 minutes or until onion is tender. Add chili powder, cumin, oregano, cinnamon, red pepper and cloves. Cook and stir 1 minute.

Add tomatoes; reduce heat to medium-low. Simmer, uncovered, 20 minutes or until sauce is reduced to 3 to 3¼ cups.   *Makes about 3 cups*

Crab and Corn Enchilada Casserole

JAZZY JAMBALAYA

1 package (6.8 ounces) RICE-A-RONI®
    Spanish Rice
1 cup chopped cooked chicken or ham
1 cup chopped onion
1 cup chopped green bell pepper
2 cloves garlic, minced
3 tablespoons vegetable oil
1 can (14½ ounces) tomatoes, undrained,
    chopped
    Dash hot pepper sauce (optional)
½ pound raw shrimp, shelled, deveined *or*
    8 ounces frozen cleaned precooked
    shrimp

1. In large skillet, combine rice-vermicelli mix, chicken, onion, green pepper, garlic and oil. Sauté over medium heat, stirring frequently, until vermicelli is golden brown.

2. Stir in 2 cups water, tomatoes, hot pepper sauce and contents of seasoning packet; bring to a boil over high heat.

3. Cover; reduce heat. Simmer 10 minutes.

4. Stir in shrimp.

5. Cover; continue cooking 8 to 10 minutes or until liquid is absorbed, rice is tender and shrimp turn pink. *Makes 5 servings*

CALIFORNIA SALMON PIE

4 eggs
1 (15½-ounce) can salmon, drained and
    flaked
1 (9-ounce) package frozen artichoke
    hearts, cooked, drained and chopped *or*
    1 (14-ounce) can artichoke hearts,
    drained and chopped
¼ cup chopped green onions
¼ cup grated Parmesan cheese
2 tablespoons margarine or butter, melted
3 tablespoons REALEMON® Lemon Juice
    from Concentrate
1½ teaspoons WYLER'S® or STEERO®
    Chicken-Flavor Instant Bouillon
1 unbaked (9-inch) pie shell
1 (8-ounce) container BORDEN® or
    MEADOW GOLD® Sour Cream, at room
    temperature
1½ teaspoons dried dill weed, crumbled

Preheat oven to 425°F. In large bowl, beat eggs; add salmon, artichokes, green onions, cheese, margarine, *1 tablespoon* ReaLemon® brand and *1 teaspoon* bouillon. Pour into pie shell. Bake 25 minutes. In small bowl, combine sour cream, remaining *2 tablespoons* ReaLemon® brand, remaining *½ teaspoon* bouillon and dill weed. Spread over salmon filling; bake 5 minutes or until set. Serve warm or chilled. Garnish as desired. Refrigerate leftovers. *Makes 1 (9–inch) pie*

Jazzy Jambalaya

— *Dazzling* —
PASTA DISHES

COUNTRY CHICKEN DINNER

¼ cup milk
2 tablespoons margarine or butter
1 package (4.7 ounces) PASTA RONI®
    Linguine Pasta with Chicken & Broccoli
2 cups frozen mixed broccoli, cauliflower
    and carrots vegetable medley
2 cups chopped cooked chicken or turkey
1 teaspoon dried basil

1. In round 3-quart microwaveable glass casserole, combine 1¾ cups water, milk and margarine. Microwave, uncovered, on HIGH 4 to 5 minutes or until boiling.

2. Gradually add pasta while stirring.

3. Stir in contents of seasoning packet, frozen vegetables, chicken and basil.

4. Microwave, uncovered, on HIGH 14 to 15 minutes, stirring gently after 7 minutes. Sauce will be thin, but will thicken upon standing.

5. Let stand 4 to 5 minutes or until desired consistency. Stir before serving.

Makes 4 servings

PASTA DISHES

HERBED ANGEL HAIR MUSHROOM WEDGE

4 cups cooked angel hair pasta
¾ cup cholesterol free egg substitute
½ cup freshly grated Parmesan cheese
2 green onions with tops, chopped
1 tablespoon chopped fresh basil
1 tablespoon chopped fresh sage
1 tablespoon chopped fresh mint
⅛ teaspoon ground black pepper
1 tablespoon olive oil
2 cups sliced fresh mushrooms
1 cup spaghetti sauce, heated

Preheat oven to 375°F. Combine pasta with egg substitute, Parmesan, onions, basil, sage, mint and black pepper in large bowl. Mix well. Set aside.

Heat oil in medium nonstick skillet over low heat. Add mushrooms; cook and stir 2 to 3 minutes or until tender. Add mushrooms to pasta mixture.

Spray 9-inch square baking pan with nonstick cooking spray. Pour pasta mixture into pan, pressing firmly until packed down. Bake 25 to 30 minutes or until crisp and lightly browned and center is firm to touch. Remove from oven; cool slightly.

Loosen pasta mixture from edges and bottom with spatula. Invert to remove from pan. Cut into wedges. Serve with spaghetti sauce.

Makes 8 servings

EASY TEX–MEX BAKE

8 ounces uncooked thin mostaccioli
　Nonstick cooking spray
1 pound ground turkey breast
1 package (10 ounces) frozen corn, thawed, drained
⅔ cup bottled medium or mild salsa
1 container (16 ounces) 1% low fat cottage cheese
1 egg
1 tablespoon minced fresh cilantro
½ teaspoon ground white pepper
¼ teaspoon ground cumin
½ cup (2 ounces) shredded Monterey Jack cheese

Cook pasta according to package directions, omitting salt. Drain and rinse well; set aside.

Spray large nonstick skillet with cooking spray. Add turkey; cook until no longer pink, about 5 minutes. Stir in corn and salsa. Remove from heat.

Preheat oven to 350°F. Combine cottage cheese, egg, cilantro, white pepper and cumin in small bowl. Spoon half of turkey mixture in bottom of 11 × 7-inch baking dish. Top with pasta. Spoon cottage cheese mixture over pasta. Top with remaining turkey mixture. Sprinkle Monterey Jack cheese over casserole. Bake 25 to 30 minutes or until heated through.

Makes 6 servings

Herbed Angel Hair Mushroom Wedge

PASTA DISHES

WISCONSIN SWISS LINGUINE TART

- ½ **cup butter, divided**
- 2 **cloves garlic, minced**
- 30 **thin French bread slices**
- 3 **tablespoons all-purpose flour**
- 1 **teaspoon salt**
- ¼ **teaspoon white pepper**
-    **Dash ground nutmeg**
- 2½ **cups milk**
- ¼ **cup grated Wisconsin Parmesan cheese**
- 2 **eggs, beaten**
- 8 **ounces fresh linguine, cooked and drained**
- 2 **cups (8 ounces) shredded Wisconsin Swiss cheese, divided**
- ⅓ **cup sliced green onions**
- 2 **tablespoons minced fresh basil** *or*
-    1 **teaspoon dried basil leaves, crushed**
- 2 **plum tomatoes, each cut lengthwise into eighths**

Preheat oven to 400°F. Melt ¼ cup butter in small saucepan over medium heat. Add garlic; cook 1 minute. Brush 10-inch pie plate with butter mixture. Line bottom and side of pie plate with bread, allowing bread to extend up to 1 inch over side of dish. Brush bread with remaining butter mixture. Bake 5 minutes or until lightly browned. *Reduce heat to 350°F.*

Melt remaining ¼ cup butter in medium saucepan over low heat. Stir in flour and seasonings. Gradually stir in milk; cook, stirring constantly, until thickened. Add Parmesan cheese. Remove small amount of sauce. Add to eggs; stir until blended. Return egg mixture to saucepan; mix well. Set aside.

Combine linguine, 1¼ cups Swiss cheese, onions and basil in large bowl. Pour sauce over linguine mixture; toss to coat. Pour into crust. Arrange tomatoes on top; sprinkle with remaining ¾ cup Swiss cheese. Bake 25 minutes or until thoroughly heated; let stand 5 minutes. Garnish as desired.

Makes 8 servings

*Favorite recipe from **Wisconsin Milk Marketing Board***

Wisconsin Swiss Linguine Tart

PASTA DISHES

SHRIMP NOODLE SUPREME

- **1 package (8 ounces) spinach noodles, cooked and drained**
- **1 package (3 ounces) cream cheese, cubed and softened**
- **1½ pounds medium shrimp, peeled and deveined**
- **½ cup butter, softened**
- **Salt and pepper to taste**
- **1 can (10¾ ounces) condensed cream of mushroom soup**
- **1 cup dairy sour cream**
- **½ cup half-and-half**
- **½ cup mayonnaise**
- **1 tablespoon chopped chives**
- **1 tablespoon chopped parsley**
- **½ teaspoon Dijon mustard**
- **¾ cup (6 ounces) shredded sharp Cheddar cheese**

Preheat oven to 325°F. Combine noodles and cream cheese in medium bowl. Spread noodle mixture on bottom of greased 13 × 9-inch glass casserole. Cook shrimp in butter in large skillet over medium-high heat until pink and tender, about 5 minutes. Season with salt and pepper. Spread shrimp over noodles.

Combine soup, sour cream, half-and-half, mayonnaise, chives, parsley and mustard in another medium bowl. Spread over shrimp. Sprinkle

Cheddar cheese over top. Bake 25 minutes or until hot and cheese is melted. Garnish with lemon slices and paprika, if desired.   *Makes 6 servings*

BAKED RIGATONI WITH SAUSAGE

- **½ pound Italian sausage***
- **2 cups low fat milk**
- **2 tablespoons all-purpose flour**
- **½ pound rigatoni pasta, cooked and drained**
- **2½ cups (10 ounces) shredded mozzarella cheese**
- **¼ cup grated Parmesan cheese**
- **1 teaspoon LAWRY'S® Garlic Salt**
- **¾ teaspoon LAWRY'S® Seasoned Pepper**
- **2 to 3 tablespoons dry bread crumbs *or***
- **¾ cup croutons**

In large skillet, crumble Italian sausage. Brown 5 minutes; drain fat. Stir in mixture of milk and flour; bring to a boil, stirring constantly. Stir in pasta, cheeses, Garlic Salt and Seasoned Pepper. Place in 1½-quart baking dish. Bake in 350°F oven 25 minutes. Sprinkle with bread crumbs; place under broiler to brown.   *Makes 6 servings*

*¼ pound cooked, diced ham can replace sausage.

Shrimp Noodle Supreme

PASTA DISHES

ENLIGHTENED MACARONI AND CHEESE

8 ounces uncooked wagon wheel, bow tie or elbow pasta
1 tablespoon all-purpose flour
2 teaspoons cornstarch
¼ teaspoon dry mustard
1 can (12 ounces) evaporated skimmed milk
1 cup (4 ounces) shredded reduced fat medium sharp Cheddar cheese
½ cup (2 ounces) shredded reduced fat Monterey Jack cheese
1 jar (2 ounces) diced pimiento, drained and rinsed
1 teaspoon Worcestershire sauce
¼ teaspoon ground black pepper
1 tablespoon dry bread crumbs
1 tablespoon paprika

Preheat oven to 375°F. Cook pasta according to package directions. Drain and set aside.

Combine flour, cornstarch and mustard in medium saucepan; stir in milk until smooth. Cook over medium heat, stirring occasionally, until slightly thickened, about 8 minutes. Remove from heat; stir in cheeses, pimiento, Worcestershire sauce and pepper. Add pasta; mix well.

Spray 1½-quart casserole with nonstick cooking spray. Spoon mixture into casserole; sprinkle with bread crumbs and paprika. Bake 20 minutes or until bubbly and heated through.

Makes 6 (1-cup) servings

POLISH REUBEN CASSEROLE

2 cans (10¾ ounces each) condensed cream of mushroom soup
1⅓ cups milk
½ cup chopped onion
1 tablespoon prepared mustard
2 cans (16 ounces each) sauerkraut, rinsed and drained
1 package (8 ounces) uncooked medium-width noodles
1½ pounds Polish sausage, cut into ½-inch pieces
2 cups (8 ounces) shredded Swiss cheese
¾ cup whole wheat bread crumbs
2 tablespoons butter, melted

Combine soup, milk, onion and mustard in medium bowl; blend well. Spread sauerkraut into greased 13 × 9-inch pan. Top with uncooked noodles. Spoon soup mixture evenly over noodles; cover with sausage. Top with cheese. Combine bread crumbs and butter in small bowl; sprinkle over cheese. Cover pan tightly with foil. Bake in preheated 350°F oven 1 hour or until noodles are tender. Garnish as desired.

Makes 8 to 10 servings

*Favorite recipe from **North Dakota Wheat Commission***

Enlightened Macaroni and Cheese

PASTA DISHES

LAYERED PASTA RICOTTA PIE

¼ (1-pound) package CREAMETTE® Vermicelli
⅓ cup finely chopped onion
4 cloves garlic, finely chopped
1 tablespoon olive or vegetable oil
1 cup grated fresh Romano cheese
3 eggs
1 (15- or 16-ounce) container ricotta cheese
1 (10-ounce) package frozen chopped spinach, thawed and well drained
½ teaspoon salt
1 (26-ounce) jar CLASSICO® Di Sicilia (Ripe Olives & Mushrooms) Pasta Sauce

Preheat oven to 350°F. Break vermicelli into thirds; cook according to package directions. Drain. Meanwhile, in large skillet, cook onion and garlic in oil until tender; remove from heat. Add cooked vermicelli, *½ cup* Romano cheese and *1 egg*; mix well. Press into well-greased 9-inch springform pan. Combine *2 egg yolks*, ricotta cheese, spinach, salt and remaining *½ cup* Romano cheese. Spread over pasta layer. In small mixer bowl, beat *2 egg whites* until stiff but not dry; fold into *1½ cups* pasta sauce. Pour over spinach mixture. Bake 50 to 60 minutes or until set; let stand 10 minutes. Heat remaining pasta sauce; serve with pie. Garnish as desired. Refrigerate leftovers. *Makes 6 to 8 servings*

ITALIAN BEEF AND PASTA

1¼ pounds boneless beef round steak (full cut) or boneless beef chuck steak, cut ½ inch thick
1 tablespoon vegetable oil
1 medium onion, chopped
1 large clove garlic, minced
1 teaspoon Italian seasoning
1 can (14½ ounces) Italian-style stewed tomatoes, undrained, chopped
1 can (13¾ ounces) beef broth
¼ cup red wine
½ pound mushrooms, halved
1½ cups (4 ounces) uncooked mostaccioli
2 tablespoons grated Parmesan cheese
1 tablespoon chopped parsley (optional)

Cut steak into 1-inch pieces. Heat oil in large skillet or Dutch oven over medium heat until hot. Add half of steak; cook and stir until browned. Pour off any drippings; discard. Set cooked steak aside. Repeat with remaining steak. Stir in onion, garlic and Italian seasoning; cook 2 minutes. Add tomatoes, broth and wine. Bring to a boil. Reduce heat to low; cover tightly and cook on top of range or in 300°F oven 1½ hours, or until meat is tender. Add mushrooms and mostaccioli, stirring to separate pasta. Cook, covered, 20 minutes. Remove cover; continue cooking 10 minutes or until mostaccioli is tender. Transfer to deep serving dish; stir in Parmesan cheese. Sprinkle with parsley, if desired. *Makes 4 servings*

Favorite recipe from **National Live Stock & Meat Board**

Layered Pasta Ricotta Pie

PASTA DISHES

RIGATONI WITH FOUR CHEESES

    3 cups milk
    1 tablespoon chopped carrot
    1 tablespoon chopped celery
    1 tablespoon chopped onion
    1 tablespoon parsley sprigs
    ½ bay leaf
    ¼ teaspoon black peppercorns
    ¼ teaspoon hot pepper sauce
        Dash ground nutmeg
    ¼ cup butter
    ¼ cup all–purpose flour
    ½ cup grated Wisconsin Parmesan cheese
    ¼ cup grated Wisconsin Romano cheese
    12 ounces uncooked rigatoni, cooked and
        drained
    1½ cups (6 ounces) shredded Wisconsin
        Cheddar cheese
    1½ cups (6 ounces) shredded Wisconsin
        mozzarella cheese
    ¼ teaspoon chili powder

Combine milk, carrot, celery, onion, parsley, bay leaf, peppercorns, hot pepper sauce and nutmeg in large saucepan. Bring to a boil. Reduce heat to low; simmer 10 minutes. Strain; reserve liquid.

Preheat oven to 350°F. Melt butter in medium saucepan over medium heat. Stir in flour. Gradually stir in reserved liquid. Cook, stirring constantly, until thickened. Remove from heat. Add Parmesan and Romano cheeses; stir until

blended. Pour into large bowl. Add rigatoni; toss gently to coat. Combine Cheddar and mozzarella cheeses in medium bowl. Place half the pasta mixture in greased 2-quart casserole; sprinkle with cheese mixture. Top with remaining pasta mixture. Sprinkle with chili powder. Bake 25 minutes or until bubbly. Garnish as desired.

Makes 6 servings

Favorite recipe from Wisconsin Milk Marketing Board

15–MINUTE PASTA COMBO

    8 ounces uncooked spaghetti, broken in
        half
    ½ cup KRAFT® House Italian Dressing
    2 large tomatoes, seeded and chopped
    2 cups LOUIS RICH® Hickory Smoked
        Breast of Turkey cubes
    1 cup (4 ounces) KRAFT® 100% Grated
        Parmesan Cheese

•Cook spaghetti according to package directions; drain.

•In same pan used to cook pasta, heat dressing over medium heat. Add pasta; toss until well coated.

•Add tomatoes, turkey and Parmesan cheese; toss lightly. Garnish as desired.   *Makes 6 servings*

Rigatoni with Four Cheeses

PASTA DISHES

PASTITSO

- 8 ounces uncooked elbow macaroni
- ½ cup cholesterol free egg substitute
- ¼ teaspoon ground nutmeg
- ¾ pound lean ground lamb, beef or turkey
- ½ cup chopped onion
- 1 clove garlic, minced
- 1 can (8 ounces) tomato sauce
- ¾ teaspoon dried mint leaves
- ½ teaspoon dried oregano leaves
- ½ teaspoon ground black pepper
- ⅛ teaspoon ground cinnamon
- 2 teaspoons reduced calorie margarine
- 3 tablespoons all-purpose flour
- 1½ cups skim milk
- 2 tablespoons grated Parmesan cheese

Cook pasta according to package directions. Drain and transfer to medium bowl; stir in egg substitute and nutmeg. Spray bottom of 9-inch square baking dish with nonstick cooking spray. Spread pasta mixture in baking dish. Set aside.

Preheat oven to 350°F. Cook lamb, onion and garlic in large nonstick skillet over medium heat until lamb is no longer pink. Stir in tomato sauce, mint, oregano, pepper and cinnamon. Reduce heat to low and simmer 10 minutes; spread over pasta.

Melt margarine in small saucepan over medium heat. Add flour. Stir 1 minute. Whisk in milk. Cook, stirring constantly, until thickened, about 6 minutes; spread over meat mixture. Sprinkle with cheese. Bake 30 to 40 minutes or until set.

Makes 6 servings

CHILI WAGON WHEEL CASSEROLE

- 8 ounces uncooked wagon wheel or other pasta
- Nonstick cooking spray
- 1 pound 95% lean ground beef or ground turkey breast
- ¾ cup chopped green bell pepper
- ¾ cup chopped onion
- 1 can (14½ ounces) no-salt-added stewed tomatoes
- 1 can (8 ounces) no-salt-added tomato sauce
- ½ teaspoon ground black pepper
- ¼ teaspoon ground allspice
- ½ cup (2 ounces) shredded reduced fat Cheddar cheese

Preheat oven to 350°F. Cook pasta according to package directions, omitting salt. Drain and rinse; set aside.

Spray large nonstick skillet with cooking spray. Add ground beef, bell pepper and onion; cook 5 minutes or until meat is no longer pink, stirring frequently. (Drain mixture if using ground beef.) Stir in tomatoes, tomato sauce, black pepper and allspice; cook 2 minutes. Stir in pasta. Spoon mixture into 2½-quart casserole. Sprinkle with cheese. Bake 20 to 25 minutes or until heated through.

Makes 6 servings

Pastitso

PASTA DISHES

ANGEL HAIR AL FRESCO

¾ cup skim milk
1 tablespoon margarine or butter
1 package (4.8 ounces) PASTA RONI® Angel
    Hair Pasta with Herbs
1 can (6⅛ ounces) white tuna in water,
    drained, flaked *or* 1½ cups chopped
    cooked chicken
2 medium tomatoes, chopped
⅓ cup sliced green onions
¼ cup dry white wine or water
¼ cup slivered almonds, toasted (optional)
1 tablespoon chopped fresh basil *or*
    1 teaspoon dried basil

1. In 3-quart saucepan, combine 1⅓ cups water, skim milk and margarine. Bring just to a boil.

2. Stir in pasta, contents of seasoning packet, tuna, tomatoes, onions, wine, almonds and basil. Return to a boil; reduce heat to medium.

3. Boil, uncovered, stirring frequently, 6 to 8 minutes. Sauce will be thin, but will thicken upon standing.

4. Let stand 3 minutes or until desired consistency. Stir before serving.   *Makes 4 servings*

SAN ANTONIO–STYLE TURKEY–PASTA SKILLET

2 large onions, coarsely chopped (2 cups)
2 cloves garlic, minced
¼ cup vegetable oil
10 ounces uncooked vermicelli, broken into
    pieces
2 cups diced cooked turkey or chicken
1 can (16 ounces) whole tomatoes,
    undrained
1 can (about 14 ounces) chicken broth
¾ cup PACE® Picante Sauce
1 teaspoon ground cumin
1 large green bell pepper, cut into short thin
    strips
½ cup (2 ounces) shredded Cheddar cheese
¼ cup chopped cilantro, optional
    Additional PACE® Picante Sauce, optional

Cook and stir onions and garlic in oil in 12-inch skillet over medium heat 2 minutes. Add pasta; cook and stir 2 minutes. Stir in turkey, tomatoes with juice, broth, ¾ cup picante sauce and cumin. Simmer, stirring occasionally and breaking up tomatoes with spoon, 3 minutes. Add green pepper; continue to simmer until pasta is tender and most of liquid is absorbed, 4 to 5 minutes. Sprinkle with cheese and cilantro. Serve with additional picante sauce and garnish, if desired.

Makes 6 servings

Angel Hair al Fresco

PASTA DISHES

TEX–MEX NOODLE CAKE

8 ounces uncooked angel hair pasta
½ cup finely chopped red bell pepper
1 whole egg plus 1 egg white
3 tablespoons grated Asiago or Parmesan cheese
2 tablespoons skim milk
2 teaspoons chili powder
½ teaspoon ground cumin
¼ teaspoon ground black pepper
Plain nonfat yogurt
Minced fresh cilantro

Cook pasta according to package directions, omitting salt. Drain and cool slightly, but do not rinse. Place pasta in medium bowl with bell pepper. Combine whole egg, egg white, cheese, milk, chili powder, cumin and black pepper in small bowl; pour over pasta, tossing to coat evenly.

Spray large nonstick skillet with nonstick cooking spray. Add pasta mixture, spreading evenly and pressing firmly. Cook over medium-low heat until bottom is golden brown, about 7 to 8 minutes.

Slide noodle cake onto large plate, invert and return noodle cake to skillet. Cook until brown, 3 to 5 minutes. Cut into wedges; serve warm, topped with yogurt and cilantro.

Makes 6 servings

PASTA WITH VEGETABLES AND CLASSICA™ ROMANO CHEESE

3 tablespoons olive oil
1 yellow bell pepper, cut into thin strips
1 small eggplant, cut into small cubes
3 medium ripe tomatoes, seeded and chopped
1 clove garlic, minced
1 tablespoon capers
5 Italian or Greek olives, pitted and chopped
5 fresh basil leaves, shredded, *or* 1 tablespoon dried basil leaves
12 ounces tube-shaped pasta, uncooked
½ cup grated CLASSICA® Brand Pecorino Romano Cheese
Ground black pepper

In large skillet, heat olive oil over medium heat. Add bell pepper, eggplant, tomatoes and garlic. Cook about 5 minutes or until eggplant and bell pepper are lightly golden. Reduce heat to low.

Add capers, olives and basil. Cover and cook until vegetables are tender, 15 to 20 minutes, stirring occasionally.

While vegetables are cooking, bring large saucepan of water to a boil. Add pasta and cook until slightly tender but still firm. Drain. Place in large serving bowl. Add vegetables and cheese; toss lightly. Season with black pepper. Mix gently; serve immediately. *Makes 4 servings*

Tex-Mex Noodle Cake

PASTA DISHES

ANGEL HAIR CARBONARA

⅔ cup milk
2 tablespoons margarine or butter
1 package (4.8 ounces) PASTA RONI® Angel Hair Pasta with Herbs
2 cups cubed cooked ham or pork
1 package (10 ounces) frozen peas
¼ cup sliced green onions

1. In round 3-quart microwaveable glass casserole, combine 1½ cups water, milk and margarine. Microwave, uncovered, on HIGH 4 to 5 minutes or until boiling.

2. Gradually add pasta while stirring. Separate pasta with fork, if needed.

3. Stir in contents of seasoning packet.

4. Microwave, uncovered, on HIGH 4 minutes, stirring gently after 2 minutes. Separate pasta with fork, if needed. Stir in pork, frozen peas and onions. Continue to microwave 2 to 3 minutes. Sauce will be thin, but will thicken upon standing.

5. Let stand 3 minutes or until desired consistency. Stir before serving.　　*Makes 4 servings*

CRAZY LASAGNA CASSEROLE

1½ pounds ground beef
1 teaspoon LAWRY'S® Seasoned Salt
1 package (1½ ounces) LAWRY'S® Original-Style Spaghetti Sauce Spices & Seasonings
1 can (8 ounces) tomato sauce
1 can (6 ounces) tomato paste
1½ cups water
1 package (10 ounces) medium-size shell macaroni, cooked and drained
1 carton (16 ounces) small curd cottage cheese
1½ cups (6 ounces) shredded Cheddar cheese

In large skillet, brown ground beef until crumbly; drain fat. Add Seasoned Salt, Original-Style Spaghetti Sauce Spices & Seasonings, tomato sauce, tomato paste and water; blend well. Bring to a boil; reduce heat and simmer, uncovered, 10 minutes, stirring occasionally. In shallow 2-quart casserole, layer half of macaroni, cottage cheese and meat sauce. Sprinkle ½ cup Cheddar cheese over meat sauce. Repeat layers, ending with remaining meat sauce. Top with remaining 1 cup Cheddar cheese. Bake, uncovered, in 350°F oven 30 to 40 minutes or until bubbly and cheese is melted.　　*Makes 8 servings*

Angel Hair Carbonara

PASTA DISHES

SKILLET PASTA ROMA

½ pound Italian sausage, sliced or crumbled
1 large onion, coarsely chopped
1 large clove garlic, minced
**2 cans (14½ ounces each) DEL MONTE®
Chunky Pasta Style Stewed Tomatoes,
undrained**
**1 can (8 ounces) DEL MONTE® Tomato
Sauce**
1 cup water
**8 ounces uncooked rotini or other spiral
pasta**
8 sliced mushrooms, optional
**Grated Parmesan cheese and fresh
parsley sprigs, optional**

In large skillet, brown sausage. Add onion and garlic. Cook until onion is soft; drain. Stir in stewed tomatoes with juice, tomato sauce, water and pasta. Cover and bring to a boil; reduce heat. Simmer, covered, 25 to 30 minutes or until pasta is tender, stirring occasionally. Stir in mushrooms, if desired; simmer 5 minutes. Serve in skillet garnished with cheese and parsley, if desired.

Makes 4 servings

PIZZA PASTA

1 medium green bell pepper, chopped
1 medium onion, chopped
1 cup sliced mushrooms
**½ teaspoon LAWRY'S® Garlic Powder with
Parsley or Garlic Salt**
1 tablespoon vegetable oil
¼ cup sliced ripe olives
**1 package (1.5 ounces) LAWRY'S® Original-
Style Spaghetti Sauce Spices &
Seasonings**
1¾ cups water
1 can (6 ounces) tomato paste
10 ounces mostaccioli, cooked and drained
3 ounces thinly sliced pepperoni
¾ cup shredded mozzarella cheese

In large skillet, sauté bell pepper, onion, mushrooms and Garlic Powder with Parsley in vegetable oil until vegetables are tender. Stir in olives, Spaghetti Sauce Spices & Seasonings, water and tomato paste; blend well. Bring sauce to a boil; reduce heat. Simmer, uncovered, 10 minutes. Add mostaccioli and pepperoni; blend well. Pour into 12 × 8 × 2-inch casserole; top with cheese. Bake at 350°F 15 minutes or until cheese is melted.

Makes 6 servings

Skillet Pasta Roma

— *Country* —

VEGETABLES & GRAINS

TABBOULEH

¾ **cup bulgur, rinsed, drained**
   Boiling water
2 **cups chopped seeded cucumbers**
1 **large tomato, seeded, chopped**
1 **cup snipped parsley**
⅓ **cup CRISCO® Oil**
⅓ **cup chopped green onions**
2 **tablespoons lemon juice**
1 **teaspoon dried mint leaves, crumbled**
2 **cloves garlic, minced**
½ **teaspoon salt**
⅛ **teaspoon white pepper**
⅛ **teaspoon ground red pepper**

Place bulgur in medium mixing bowl. Add enough boiling water to just cover bulgur. Let stand about 1 hour or until bulgur is rehydrated. Drain.

Combine bulgur, cucumber, tomato and parsley in large serving bowl; set aside. Blend remaining ingredients in small bowl. Pour over bulgur mixture; toss to coat. Cover; refrigerate at least 3 hours. Stir before serving.   *Makes 10 to 12 servings*

VEGETABLES & GRAINS

FRESH VEGETABLE LASAGNA

8 ounces uncooked lasagna noodles
1 package (10 ounces) frozen chopped
**   spinach, thawed, well drained**
1 cup shredded carrots
½ cup sliced green onions
½ cup sliced red bell pepper
¼ cup chopped fresh parsley
½ teaspoon ground black pepper
1½ cups low fat cottage cheese
1 cup buttermilk
½ cup plain nonfat yogurt
2 egg whites
1 cup sliced mushrooms
1 can (14 ounces) artichoke hearts, drained
**   and chopped**
2 cups (8 ounces) shredded part-skim
**   mozzarella cheese**
¼ cup freshly grated Parmesan cheese

Cook pasta according to package directions, omitting salt. Drain. Rinse under cold water; drain well. Set aside.

Preheat oven to 375°F. Pat spinach with paper towels to remove excess moisture. Combine spinach, carrots, green onions, bell pepper, parsley and black pepper in large bowl. Set aside. Combine cottage cheese, buttermilk, yogurt and egg whites in food processor or blender; process until smooth.

Spray 13 × 9-inch baking pan with nonstick cooking spray. Arrange half of lasagna noodles in bottom of pan. Spread with half each of cottage cheese mixture, vegetable mixture, mushrooms, artichokes and mozzarella. Repeat layers, ending with noodles. Sprinkle with Parmesan. Cover and bake 30 minutes. Remove cover; continue baking 20 minutes or until bubbly and heated through. Let stand 10 minutes before serving.

Makes 8 servings

DELUXE POTATO BAKE

2 eggs, beaten
¼ cup unseasoned dry bread crumbs
2 green onions with tops, chopped
2 tablespoons milk
¾ teaspoon LAWRY'S® Seasoned Pepper
½ teaspoon LAWRY'S® Seasoned Salt
2 large potatoes, peeled, grated and held in
**   ice water**
1 cup (4 ounces) shredded Cheddar cheese
4 slices cooked and crumbled bacon

In large bowl, combine eggs, bread crumbs, onions, milk, Seasoned Pepper and Seasoned Salt. Drain potatoes and stir into egg mixture. Add half of Cheddar cheese and half of bacon. Spoon mixture into lightly greased 8-inch square casserole. Bake, uncovered, in 350°F oven for 20 minutes. Sprinkle with remaining cheese and bacon; bake 5 minutes longer. *Makes 4 servings*

Fresh Vegetable Lasagna

VEGETABLES & GRAINS

VEGETABLE RISOTTO

2 cups broccoli flowerets
1 cup finely chopped zucchini
1 cup finely chopped yellow squash
1 cup finely chopped red bell pepper
2½ cups chicken broth
1 tablespoon extra virgin olive oil
2 tablespoons finely chopped onion
½ cup Arborio or other short-grain rice
¼ cup dry white wine or water
⅓ cup freshly grated Parmesan cheese

Steam broccoli, zucchini, yellow squash and bell pepper 3 minutes or just until crisp-tender. Rinse with cold water; drain and set aside.

Bring broth to a simmer in small saucepan; keep hot on low heat. Heat oil in large heavy saucepan over medium-high heat until hot. Add onion; reduce heat to medium. Cook and stir about 5 minutes or until onion is translucent. Add rice, stirring to coat with oil. Add wine; cook and stir until almost dry. Add ½ cup hot broth; cook and stir until broth is absorbed. Continue adding broth, ½ cup at a time, allowing broth to absorb before each addition and stirring frequently. (Total cooking time for broth absorption is about 20 minutes.)

Remove from heat and stir in cheese. Add steamed vegetables and mix well. Serve immediately.

Makes 6 servings

BLAZING BANDITO VEGGIE MEDLEY

1 (12-ounce) package rotini or corkscrew pasta
2 tablespoons olive oil
2 small yellow squash (6 ounces each), sliced
2 small zucchini (6 ounces each), sliced
1 small eggplant (1 pound), cut into ½-inch pieces
1 medium onion, sliced
1 medium green bell pepper, seeded and sliced
1 (8-ounce) package fresh mushrooms, sliced
1 (26-ounce) jar NEWMAN'S OWN® Bandito Diavolo Sauce
Grated Parmesan cheese (optional)

Prepare pasta according to package directions. Drain; keep warm. Meanwhile, heat olive oil in 12-inch skillet over medium-high heat. Add vegetables; cook until lightly browned and tender, about 15 minutes, stirring often.

Stir in Newman's Own® Bandito Diavolo Sauce; heat to boiling. Reduce heat to low; cover and simmer 10 minutes to blend flavors. Spoon sauce over pasta on warm large platter; toss to serve. Serve with grated Parmesan cheese.

Makes 4 servings

Vegetable Risotto

VEGETABLES & GRAINS

ZUCCHINI TOMATO BAKE

- 1 pound eggplant, coarsely chopped
- 2 cups thinly sliced zucchini
- 2 cups sliced fresh mushrooms
- 2 teaspoons olive oil
- ½ cup chopped onion
- ½ cup chopped fresh fennel
- 2 cloves garlic, minced
- 1 can (14½ ounces) no-salt-added whole tomatoes, undrained
- 1 tablespoon no-salt-added tomato paste
- 2 teaspoons dried basil leaves
- 1 teaspoon sugar

Preheat oven to 350°F. Arrange eggplant, zucchini and mushrooms in 9-inch square baking dish.

Heat oil in small skillet over medium heat. Cook and stir onion, fennel and garlic 3 to 4 minutes or until onion is tender. Add tomatoes, tomato paste, basil and sugar. Cook and stir about 4 minutes or until sauce thickens.

Pour sauce over eggplant mixture. Cover and bake 30 minutes. Cool slightly before serving. Garnish as desired. *Makes 6 servings*

CHILI BEAN RAGOÛT

- 1 cup chopped onions
- 1 cup sliced celery
- 1 cup cubed green peppers
- 2 cloves garlic, minced
- 3 to 4 teaspoons chili powder
- 1 teaspoon dried oregano leaves
- 1 teaspoon dried basil leaves
- ½ teaspoon dried thyme leaves
- 1 can (17 ounces) lima beans, drained
- 1 can (16 ounces) no-salt-added whole tomatoes, undrained, coarsely chopped
- 1 can (15½ ounces) kidney beans, drained
- 1 can (16 ounces) ½-less-salt whole kernel corn, drained
- 1 can (15 ounces) black-eyed peas, drained
- Hot cooked rice or cornbread

Spray bottom of large saucepan with nonstick cooking spray; heat over high heat. Cook and stir onions, celery, green peppers and garlic until tender. Stir in chili powder, oregano, basil and thyme; cook 1 minute. Stir in lima beans, tomatoes with juice, kidney beans, corn and black-eyed peas; heat to boiling. Reduce heat and simmer, uncovered, 10 minutes. Serve over rice or cornbread. *Makes 8 servings*

*Favorite recipe from **Canned Food Information Council***

Zucchini Tomato Bake

HARVEST VEGETABLE SCALLOP

- **4 medium carrots, thinly sliced**
- **1 package (10 ounces) frozen chopped broccoli, thawed and drained**
- **1 can (2.8 ounces) FRENCH'S® French Fried Onions**
- **5 small red potatoes, sliced ⅛ inch thick**
- **1 jar (8 ounces) pasteurized processed cheese spread**
- **¼ cup milk**
- **Freshly ground black pepper**
- **Seasoned salt**

Preheat oven to 375°F. In 8 × 12-inch baking dish, combine carrots, broccoli and *½ can* French Fried Onions. Tuck potato slices into vegetable mixture at an angle. Dot vegetables evenly with cheese spread. Pour milk over vegetables; sprinkle with seasonings as desired. Bake, covered, at 375°F for 30 minutes or until vegetables are tender. Top with remaining onions; bake, uncovered, 3 minutes or until onions are golden brown.

Makes 6 servings

MICROWAVE DIRECTIONS: In 8 × 12-inch microwave-safe dish, prepare vegetables as above. Top with cheese spread, milk and seasonings as above. Cook, covered, on HIGH 12 to 14 minutes or until vegetables are tender, rotating dish halfway through cooking time. Top with remaining onions; cook, uncovered, 1 minute. Let stand 5 minutes.

POTATO GORGONZOLA GRATIN

- **1 pound (2 medium-large) COLORADO BAKING POTATOES, unpeeled, very thinly sliced, divided**
- **Salt**
- **Pepper**
- **Ground nutmeg**
- **½ medium onion, thinly sliced**
- **1 medium tart green apple, such as pippin or Granny Smith, *or* 1 medium pear, unpeeled, cored, very thinly sliced**
- **1 cup low-fat milk or half-and-half**
- **¾ cup (3 ounces) Gorgonzola or other blue cheese, crumbled**
- **2 tablespoons freshly grated Parmesan cheese**

Preheat oven to 400°F. In 8- or 9-inch square baking dish, arrange half the potatoes. Season generously with salt and pepper; sprinkle lightly with nutmeg. Top with onion and apple. Arrange remaining potatoes on top. Season again with salt and pepper; add milk. Cover dish with aluminum foil. Bake 30 to 40 minutes or until potatoes are tender. Remove foil; top with both cheeses. Bake, uncovered, 10 to 15 minutes or until top is lightly browned. *Makes 4 to 6 servings*

*Favorite recipe from **Colorado Potato Administrative Committee***

CARIBBEAN VEGETARIAN CURRY

 3 firm, medium DOLE® Bananas, peeled
 3 teaspoons margarine, divided
 1 onion, halved, thinly sliced
 2 large cloves garlic, pressed
 1 tart apple, peeled, cored, chopped
 1½ teaspoons curry powder
 1½ teaspoons grated lemon peel
 1 teaspoon *each:* ground ginger, ground coriander
 ⅛ teaspoon *each:* turmeric, ground red pepper
 1 can (15 ounces) black-eyed peas, drained
 1 can (15 ounces) kidney beans, undrained
 ⅓ cup DOLE® Raisins
 1 cup plain nonfat yogurt
 3 warm hard-cooked eggs, halved
 3 cups hot cooked rice (about 1 cup uncooked)
 6 DOLE® Radishes, thinly sliced
 3 DOLE® Green Onions, thinly sliced
 ½ cup chopped fresh cilantro
 ¼ cup chopped peanuts

•Cut bananas in half crosswise, then lengthwise in half to make 12 pieces. Cook and stir in nonstick skillet with 2 teaspoons margarine until lightly browned. Remove to plate.

•Add remaining 1 teaspoon margarine to skillet. Cook and stir onion, garlic and apple until soft.

•Combine curry powder, lemon peel, ginger, coriander, turmeric and red pepper. Stir into onion mixture.

•Add black-eyed peas, undrained kidney beans and raisins. Cover; simmer 5 minutes. Remove from heat; stir in yogurt.

•On individual serving plates, place egg halves on rice. Surround with cooked bananas. Spoon curry-vegetable mixture over rice. Top with radishes, green onions, cilantro and peanuts.

Makes 6 servings

"WILD" BLACK BEANS

 2 cups cooked wild rice
 1 can (15 ounces) black beans, undrained
 1 cup canned or thawed frozen corn, drained
 ½ cup chopped red bell pepper
 1 small jalapeño pepper, seeded and chopped
 1 tablespoon red wine vinegar
 1 cup (4 ounces) shredded Monterey Jack cheese
 ¼ cup chopped fresh cilantro

Preheat oven to 350°F. In 1½-quart baking dish, combine wild rice, beans, corn, bell pepper, jalapeño and vinegar. Cover; bake 20 minutes. Top with cheese; bake, uncovered, 10 minutes. Garnish with cilantro. *Makes 6 to 8 servings*

*Favorite recipe from **Minnesota Cultivated Wild Rice Council***

DOUBLE SPINACH BAKE

1 cup fresh mushroom slices

1 green onion with top, finely chopped

1 clove garlic, minced

4 to 5 cups fresh spinach, coarsely chopped *or* 1 package (10 ounces) frozen spinach, thawed and drained

1 tablespoon water

1 container (15 ounces) nonfat ricotta cheese

¼ cup skim milk

1 egg

½ teaspoon ground nutmeg

½ teaspoon ground black pepper

8 ounces spinach fettuccine, cooked and drained

¼ cup (1 ounce) shredded reduced fat Swiss cheese

Preheat oven to 350°F. Spray medium skillet with nonstick cooking spray. Add mushrooms, green onion and garlic. Cook and stir over medium heat until mushrooms are softened. Add spinach and water. Cover; cook until spinach is wilted, about 3 minutes.

Combine ricotta cheese, milk, egg, nutmeg and black pepper in large bowl. Gently stir in noodles and vegetables; toss to coat evenly. Lightly coat shallow 1½-quart casserole with nonstick cooking spray. Spread noodle mixture in casserole. Sprinkle with Swiss cheese. Bake 25 to 30 minutes or until knife inserted halfway to center comes out clean.

Makes 6 (1-cup) servings

BROCCOLI CASSEROLE WITH CRUMB TOPPING

2 slices day-old white bread, coarsely crumbled (about 1¼ cups)

½ cup (2 ounces) shredded mozzarella cheese

2 tablespoons chopped fresh parsley (optional)

2 tablespoons olive or vegetable oil

1 small clove garlic, finely chopped

6 cups broccoli florets and/or cauliflowerets

1 envelope LIPTON® Recipe Secrets® Onion Soup Mix

1 cup water

1 large tomato, diced

In small bowl, combine bread crumbs, cheese, parsley, 1 tablespoon oil and garlic; set aside.

In 12-inch skillet, heat remaining 1 tablespoon oil over medium heat and cook broccoli, stirring frequently, 2 minutes. Stir in Onion Soup Mix blended with water. Bring to a boil over high heat. Reduce heat to low and simmer uncovered, stirring occasionally, 8 minutes or until broccoli is almost tender. Add tomato; simmer an additional 2 minutes. Spoon vegetable mixture into 2-quart ovenproof baking dish; top with bread crumb mixture. Broil 1½ minutes or until crumbs are golden and cheese is melted.

Makes about 6 servings

Double Spinach Bake

VEGETABLES & GRAINS

ORIGINAL GREEN BEAN CASSEROLE

2 cans (16 ounces each) cut green beans, drained *or* 2 packages (9 ounces each) frozen cut green beans, cooked and drained
¾ cup milk
1 can (10¾ ounces) condensed cream of mushroom soup
⅛ teaspoon freshly ground black pepper
1 can (2.8 ounces) FRENCH'S® French Fried Onions

Preheat oven to 350°F. In medium bowl, combine beans, milk, soup, pepper and ½ can French Fried Onions; pour into 1½-quart casserole. Bake, uncovered, at 350°F for 30 minutes or until heated through. Top with remaining onions; bake, uncovered, 5 minutes or until onions are golden brown. *Makes 6 servings*

MICROWAVE DIRECTIONS: Prepare green bean mixture as above; pour into 1¹/₂-quart microwave-safe casserole. Cook, covered, on HIGH 8 to 10 minutes or until heated through, stirring beans halfway through cooking time. Top with remaining onions; cook, uncovered, 1 minute. Let stand 5 minutes.

SWISS VEGETABLE MEDLEY

1 package (16 ounces) frozen vegetable combination (broccoli, carrots, cauliflower), thawed and drained
1 can (10¾ ounces) condensed cream of mushroom soup
1 cup (4 ounces) shredded Swiss cheese
⅓ cup sour cream
¼ teaspoon freshly ground black pepper
1 jar (4 ounces) diced pimiento, drained (optional)
1 can (2.8 ounces) FRENCH'S® French Fried Onions

Preheat oven to 350°F. In large bowl, combine vegetables, soup, *½ cup* cheese, sour cream, pepper, pimiento and *½ can* French Fried Onions. Pour into shallow 1-quart casserole. Bake, covered, at 350°F for 30 minutes or until vegetables are tender. Sprinkle remaining cheese and onions in diagonal rows across top; bake, uncovered, 5 minutes or until onions are golden brown. *Makes 6 servings*

MICROWAVE DIRECTIONS: Prepare vegetable mixture as above; pour into shallow 1-quart microwave-safe casserole. Cook, covered, on HIGH 8 to 10 minutes or until vegetables are tender, stirring vegetables halfway through cooking time. Top with remaining cheese and onions; cook, uncovered, 1 minute or until cheese is melted. Let stand 5 minutes.

Top to bottom: Original Green Bean Casserole; Swiss Vegetable Medley

VEGETABLES & GRAINS

FENNEL WITH PARMESAN BREAD CRUMBS

2 large fennel bulbs
½ cup dry bread crumbs
¼ cup lemon juice
1 tablespoon freshly grated Parmesan cheese
1 tablespoon capers
2 teaspoons olive oil
⅛ teaspoon ground black pepper
½ cup ⅓-less-salt chicken broth

Preheat oven to 375°F. Spray 9-inch square baking dish with nonstick cooking spray; set aside.

Remove outer leaves and wide base from fennel bulbs. Slice bulbs crosswise. Combine fennel and ¼ cup water in medium nonstick skillet with tight-fitting lid. Bring to a boil over high heat; reduce heat to medium. Cover and steam 4 minutes or until fennel is crisp-tender. Cool slightly; arrange in prepared baking pan.

Combine bread crumbs, lemon juice, Parmesan, capers, oil and black pepper in small bowl. Sprinkle bread crumb mixture over fennel; pour broth over top. Bake, uncovered, 20 to 25 minutes or until golden brown. Garnish with minced fennel leaves and red bell pepper strips, if desired.

Makes 4 servings

LAYERED VEGETABLE BAKE

2 slices day-old white bread, crumbled
2 tablespoons chopped fresh parsley (optional)
2 tablespoons margarine or butter, melted
1 large all-purpose potato (about ½ pound), thinly sliced
1 large yellow or red bell pepper, sliced
1 envelope LIPTON® Recipe Secrets® Savory Herb with Garlic or Golden Onion Soup Mix
1 large tomato, sliced

Preheat oven to 375°F.

Spray 1½-quart round casserole or baking dish with nonstick cooking spray. In small bowl, combine bread, parsley and margarine; set aside.

In prepared baking dish, arrange potato slices; top with bell pepper. Sprinkle soup mix over top. Arrange tomato slices over pepper, overlapping slightly. Sprinkle with bread mixture. Cover with aluminum foil and bake 45 minutes. Remove foil and continue baking 15 minutes or until vegetables are tender.

Makes about 6 servings

Fennel with Parmesan Bread Crumbs

— *Hearty* —
INTERNATIONAL FARE

FRENCH BEEF STEW

1½ pounds stew beef, cut into 1-inch cubes
¼ cup all-purpose flour
2 tablespoons vegetable oil
  Salt and pepper (optional)
2 cans (14½ ounces each) DEL MONTE®
  Original Style Stewed Tomatoes
1 can (14 ounces) beef broth
4 medium carrots, pared, cut into 1-inch
  chunks
2 medium potatoes, pared, cut into 1-inch
  chunks
¾ teaspoon dried thyme
2 tablespoons Dijon mustard (optional)
  Chopped parsley (optional)

Combine meat and flour in plastic bag; toss to coat evenly. In 6-quart saucepan, brown meat in oil. Season with salt and pepper, if desired. Add remaining ingredients, except mustard and parsley. Bring to boil; reduce heat. Cover and simmer 1 hour or until beef is tender. Blend in mustard, if desired. Garnish with chopped parsley, if desired. *Makes 6 to 8 servings*

INTERNATIONAL FARE

CHICKEN MEXICANA CASSEROLE

2½ pounds boned chicken breasts, skinned and cut into 1-inch cubes

2 packages (1.25 ounces each) LAWRY'S® Taco Spices & Seasonings

2 cans (14½ ounces each) whole tomatoes, undrained and cut up

3 cups (12 ounces) shredded sharp Cheddar cheese, divided

1 can (7 ounces) diced green chiles, undrained

1 can (12 ounces) whole kernel corn, drained

1 package (8¼ ounces) corn muffin mix

2 eggs

¼ cup dairy sour cream

In large bowl, toss chicken cubes with Taco Spices & Seasonings and tomatoes; blend well. Add 1 cup cheese. Spread mixture evenly into 13 × 9 × 2-inch baking dish. Spoon chiles over chicken mixture; sprinkle with remaining cheese. Set aside. In medium bowl, combine remaining ingredients; blend well. Drop by rounded spoonfuls on top of casserole, spacing evenly. Bake in 350°F oven 50 to 60 minutes or until top is lightly browned and sauce is bubbly. Remove from oven and let stand about 20 minutes before serving.

Makes 10 to 12 servings

RED CHILI TORTILLA TORTE

2 cans (16 ounces) pinto or black beans, rinsed and drained

¼ cup low-salt chicken broth

1 tablespoon vegetable oil

2 large onions, sliced

2 red bell peppers, cut into ¼-inch strips

2 zucchini, thinly sliced

2 cloves garlic, minced

1 cup corn

1 teaspoon ground cumin

½ teaspoon salt

¼ teaspoon cayenne pepper

6 (8-inch) flour tortillas

2 cups NEWMAN'S OWN® All Natural Salsa

2 cups (8 ounces) shredded Monterey Jack cheese

In food processor, process pinto beans and chicken broth until smooth; set aside.

Heat oil in large, nonstick skillet over medium heat. Add onions, bell peppers, zucchini and garlic; sauté until softened, 10 to 12 minutes. Add corn and seasonings; cook about 2 minutes.

Heat oven to 375°F. Grease 8-inch round baking dish. Spread ½ cup bean mixture onto tortilla; place in dish. Spoon 1 cup onion mixture over beans. Spoon ⅓ cup NEWMAN'S OWN® All Natural Salsa over onion mixture; top with ⅓ cup cheese. Repeat layers, ending with cheese. Bake until heated through, about 45 minutes. Cut into wedges.

Makes 8 to 10 servings

Chicken Mexicana Casserole

INTERNATIONAL FARE

PACE–SETTING ENCHILADA CASSEROLE

1½ **pounds lean ground beef**
1 **small onion, chopped**
1 **garlic clove, minced**
1½ **cups PACE® picante sauce**
1 **package (10 ounces) frozen chopped spinach, thawed and squeezed dry**
1 **can (8 ounces) tomato sauce**
2 **medium tomatoes, seeded and chopped**
1 **large red bell pepper, diced**
1 **tablespoon lime juice**
1½ **teaspoons salt**
12 **corn tortillas**
1 **cup dairy sour cream**
¾ **cup (3 ounces) shredded Monterey Jack cheese**
¾ **cup (3 ounces) shredded Cheddar or additional Monterey Jack cheese**
Shredded lettuce (optional)
½ **cup sliced ripe olives**

Brown meat with onion and garlic in large skillet; drain. Add picante sauce, spinach, tomato sauce, tomatoes, bell pepper, lime juice and salt. Simmer, uncovered, 15 minutes, stirring occasionally. Arrange 6 tortillas on bottom and up sides of lightly greased 13 × 9 × 2-inch baking dish, overlapping as necessary. Top with half the meat mixture. Arrange remaining tortillas over meat mixture, overlapping as necessary. Spread sour cream evenly over tortillas. Top with remaining meat mixture.* Bake at 350°F about 30 minutes or until hot and bubbly. Remove from oven; sprinkle with both cheeses. Let stand 10 minutes; cut into squares to serve. Garnish with lettuce, if desired, and olives. Serve with additional picante sauce.

Makes 8 servings

*Note: At this point, casserole may be refrigerated up to 6 hours. Let stand at room temperature 30 minutes before baking.

FRENCH VEAL CASSEROLE

1 **pound veal steaks**
2 **tablespoons vegetable oil**
1 **cup rice**
1 **tablespoon chopped onion**
2¼ **cups water**
2 **teaspoons salt**
2 **tablespoons chopped pimiento**
½ **cup BLUE DIAMOND® Slivered Almonds, toasted**

Cut veal into ½-inch cubes. Brown lightly in oil. Remove veal from pan. Combine rice and onion in same pan and cook, stirring, until rice is golden brown. Add water and salt and bring to boil. Stir in veal. Turn into casserole dish; cover. Bake at 300°F 50 to 60 minutes or until rice and veal are tender. Just before serving, add pimiento and almonds; fluff rice with fork.

Makes 6 servings

Pace-Setting Enchilada Casserole

MEXICAN CHEESE–RICE PIE

4 eggs, divided
2 cups cooked instant brown rice
1 cup (4 ounces) shredded Cheddar cheese,
   divided
1 can (4 ounces) chopped green chilies,
   drained
1 can (12 ounces) evaporated milk
2 tablespoons chopped green onion
½ teaspoon ground cumin
¼ teaspoon salt
1 cup shredded iceberg lettuce
¼ cup prepared chunky salsa
¼ cup sliced ripe olives

In medium bowl beat 1 egg; add rice and mix well. In 9-inch glass pie plate, press rice mixture firmly on bottom and up side. Microwave on MEDIUM (50% power) about 3 to 4 minutes or until set. Sprinkle with ¾ cup Cheddar cheese and chilies; set aside.

In 1-quart glass measure or microwavable bowl combine remaining 3 eggs, milk, green onion, cumin and salt. Microwave on MEDIUM-HIGH (75% power) about 4 minutes or until hot, stirring occasionally. Pour into prepared crust; cover loosely with waxed paper.

Microwave on MEDIUM-HIGH 10 to 12 minutes or until center is almost set, rotating ½ turn after 5 minutes. Uncover; let stand 10 minutes. Remove pie from pie plate to serving platter. Arrange lettuce around edge of pie; top with salsa, olives and remaining Cheddar cheese.

Makes 6 servings

Favorite recipe from **National Dairy Board**

ORIENTAL BEEF AND BROCCOLI

½ cup HEINZ® Chili Sauce
½ teaspoon Oriental sesame oil
¼ to ½ teaspoon crushed red pepper
1 (1-pound) flank steak
2 tablespoons soy sauce
2 teaspoons cornstarch
2 cups broccoli flowerets
1 medium red bell pepper, cut into strips
1 medium onion, cut into thin wedges
1 tablespoon vegetable oil
1 can (8 ounces) sliced water chestnuts,
   drained

Combine chili sauce, sesame oil and crushed red pepper; set aside. Cut flank steak lengthwise in half, then cut across the grain into thin slices. Combine soy sauce and cornstarch; pour over steak and toss to coat. In large skillet or wok, cook broccoli, bell pepper and onion in vegetable oil until tender-crisp; remove. In same skillet, quickly cook steak over high heat in 2 batches. Return steak and vegetables to skillet; stir in reserved chili sauce mixture and water chestnuts.

Makes 4 servings

Mexican Cheese-Rice Pie

INTERNATIONAL FARE

MAIN DISH MOROCCAN RICE

½ cup chopped onion
1 tablespoon olive oil
2 cups uncooked brown rice
4 cups chicken broth
1 cup diagonally sliced carrots
3 cups fresh mushroom slices
1½ teaspoons grated orange peel
¼ to ½ teaspoon ground cinnamon
⅛ teaspoon ground white pepper
2 cups red or green California seedless grapes
1 tablespoon chopped parsley

Cook and stir onion in olive oil until tender; stir in rice and cook 2 minutes. Add broth, carrots, mushrooms, orange peel, cinnamon and pepper. Cover; simmer 40 minutes. Stir in grapes and parsley; cover and simmer 5 minutes or until rice is tender.   *Makes 4 servings*

*Favorite recipe from **California Table Grape Commission***

HEARTY KIELBASA DINNER

1 cup chopped onions
3 tablespoons dried oregano
2 teaspoons ground black pepper
2 teaspoons chili powder
1 teaspoon ground red pepper
3 cloves garlic, minced
2 teaspoons vegetable oil
½ pound turkey kielbasa, thinly sliced
1 can (28 ounces) cannellini or navy beans, rinsed and drained
1 can (28 ounces) whole tomatoes, undrained
1 tablespoon plus 1 teaspoon sugar
1 package (10 ounces) frozen, chopped broccoli, thawed and drained
2 cups cooked macaroni or rice (optional)

In large skillet, cook and stir onions, oregano, black pepper, chili powder, red pepper and garlic in oil 5 minutes or until onions are tender. Add kielbasa, beans, tomatoes and sugar. Simmer 15 minutes. Add broccoli and simmer 5 minutes. Serve over macaroni or rice, if desired.
Makes 4 servings

LOVE AND QUICHES TOMATO HERB QUICHE

CRUST
9-inch Classic Crisco® Single Crust (page 10)
½ teaspoon McCORMICK®/SCHILLING® Garlic Salt
1 egg, beaten

FILLING
5 very thin slices sweet onion
¼ cup plus 1 tablespoon olive oil, divided
1 cup (4 ounces) shredded mozzarella cheese
2 cups loosely packed fresh basil leaves
½ teaspoon salt
½ teaspoon McCORMICK®/SCHILLING® Ground Black Pepper
1 clove garlic, halved
4 eggs
½ cup half-and-half
½ cup ricotta cheese
½ cup plus 1 tablespoon freshly grated Parmesan cheese, divided
6 to 8 thin slices tomato

1. For crust, heat oven to 375°F. Follow steps 6 and 7 from page 10, adding garlic salt to flour mixture. Roll and press crust into 9-inch quiche dish or glass pie plate. Brush edge of pie crust with beaten egg. Bake 10 minutes or until set and lightly browned. Cool while preparing filling. *Reduce oven temperature to 350°F.*

2. For filling, cook and stir onion in 1 tablespoon oil in small skillet on medium heat until softened. Spoon into cooled baked pie crust. Sprinkle with mozzarella cheese.

3. Combine remaining ¼ cup oil, basil, salt, pepper and garlic in blender. Blend at high speed until smooth.

4. Beat eggs in large bowl at medium speed of electric mixer until foamy. Reduce speed to low. Add half-and-half, ricotta cheese and ½ cup Parmesan cheese. Beat until well blended. Add basil mixture slowly, beating until well blended. Pour over mozzarella cheese in pie crust.

5. Bake at 350°F for 20 minutes. Remove quiche from oven. Top with tomato slices. Return quiche to oven. Bake 30 minutes or until center is firm. Sprinkle tomatoes with remaining 1 tablespoon Parmesan cheese. Serve hot, warm or cold. Refrigerate leftovers.

Makes one 9-inch quiche (8 servings)

ORZO CASSEROLE

2 tablespoons margarine or butter
1 clove garlic, finely chopped
1½ cups uncooked orzo pasta
1 envelope LIPTON® Recipe Secrets® Onion
    or Onion-Mushroom Soup Mix
3¼ cups water
6 ounces shiitake or white mushrooms,
    sliced
¼ cup chopped fresh parsley

In 3-quart heavy saucepan, melt margarine over medium heat and cook garlic with orzo, stirring constantly, 2½ minutes or until golden. Stir in onion soup mix blended with water. Bring to a boil over high heat. Reduce heat to low and simmer, covered, 10 minutes. Add mushrooms; do not stir. Simmer, covered, 10 minutes. Stir in parsley. Turn into serving bowl. (Liquid will not be totally absorbed.) Let stand 10 minutes or until liquid is absorbed. *Makes about 10 (¹/₂-cup) servings*

Savory Orzo Casserole: Increase water to 4 cups and use LIPTON® Recipe Secrets® Savory Herb with Garlic Soup Mix.

BEEF TAMALE PIE

12 ounces cooked beef, cut into ½-inch
    pieces (about 2½ cups)
1 can (15¾ ounces) chili beans in mild chili
    sauce
1 can (4 ounces) chopped green chilies,
    undrained
¼ cup sliced green onion
¼ teaspoon *each:* ground cumin and ground
    black pepper
1 package (8½ ounces) corn muffin mix
1 cup cold water
½ cup (2 ounces) shredded sharp Cheddar
    cheese

Preheat oven to 425°F. Combine beef, chili beans, chilies, green onion, cumin and pepper; mix well. Set aside. Combine corn muffin mix and water (mixture will be very thin). Grease bottom and sides of 9-inch square baking pan or 10-inch metal skillet. Pour corn muffin batter into pan. Spoon beef mixture into center of corn muffin mixture, leaving 1-inch border. Bake 30 minutes or until corn muffin mixture is slightly browned and begins to pull away from edge of pan. Sprinkle with cheese; let stand 5 minutes before serving.

Makes 4 servings

Favorite recipe from **National Live Stock & Meat Board**

Orzo Casserole

ENCHILADAS SUISSE

1 package (1.62 ounces) LAWRY'S® Spices & Seasonings for Enchilada Sauce
1 can (6 ounces) tomato paste
3 cups water
2 tablespoons vegetable oil
1 onion, finely chopped
⅛ teaspoon LAWRY'S® Garlic Powder with Parsley
3 cups shredded cooked chicken
2 tablespoons diced green chiles (optional)
LAWRY'S® Seasoned Salt to taste
LAWRY'S® Seasoned Pepper to taste
3 chicken bouillon cubes
2 cups whipping cream
12 corn tortillas
Vegetable oil for frying
8 ounces shredded Monterey Jack cheese

Prepare Spices & Seasonings for Enchilada Sauce with tomato paste and water according to package directions. In large skillet, heat oil and sauté onion and Garlic Powder with Parsley until onion is tender. Add 2 cups enchilada sauce, chicken, chiles, Seasoned Salt and Seasoned Pepper; simmer, uncovered, 5 minutes. Pour remaining enchilada sauce in bottom of 13 × 9 × 2-inch baking dish; set aside. Meanwhile, in medium saucepan, combine bouillon cubes and cream; heat until bouillon dissolves. Keep warm. To assemble enchiladas, soften each tortilla in hot oil and dip in hot cream mixture. Place ¼ cup chicken mixture on each tortilla and roll up. Place, seam side down, on sauce in baking dish. Pour remaining cream mixture over enchiladas and top with cheese. Bake, uncovered, in 350°F oven 20 to 25 minutes.

Makes 6 to 8 servings

BASQUE BEAN CASSEROLE

1 pound dried beans (Great Northern, yellow eye or pinto)
4½ cups cold water
¼ pound unsliced bacon or salt pork
2 medium leeks, thinly sliced
2 cups chopped onions
1 medium onion
6 whole cloves
1 can (13¾ ounces) chicken broth
5 carrots, cut into 1-inch slices
3 cloves garlic, minced
2 teaspoons TABASCO® pepper sauce
1 teaspoon dried thyme leaves
1 teaspoon dried marjoram leaves
1 teaspoon dried sage leaves
2 bay leaves
6 whole black peppercorns
1 can (16 ounces) whole tomatoes, crushed
1 pound Polish sausage, cut into 1-inch slices

In 6-quart Dutch oven or saucepan, combine beans and water. Let soak 2 hours. Do *not* drain beans. Meanwhile, in skillet over medium heat, brown bacon on both sides. Remove. Add leeks and chopped onions. Cook 10 minutes. Add to

soaked beans. Stud whole onion with cloves. Add onion, chicken broth, carrots, garlic, TABASCO, thyme, marjoram, sage, bay leaves and peppercorns. Bring to boil. Reduce heat and simmer, covered, 1 hour. Stir in tomatoes and sausage. Cover; bake in preheated 350°F oven 1 hour or until almost all liquid is absorbed.

Makes 6 to 8 servings

CHILAQUILES

- 1 medium onion, chopped
- 2 tablespoons vegetable oil
- 1 can (28 ounces) whole tomatoes, cut up
- 1 package (1.25 ounces) LAWRY'S® Taco Spices & Seasonings
- 1 can (4 ounces) diced green chiles (optional)
- 6 ounces tortilla chips
- 4 cups (16 ounces) grated Monterey Jack cheese
- 1 cup dairy sour cream
- ½ cup (2 ounces) grated Cheddar cheese

In large skillet, sauté onion in oil. Add tomatoes, Taco Spices & Seasonings and chiles; blend well. Simmer, uncovered, 10 to 15 minutes. In lightly greased 2-quart casserole, layer ½ of tortilla chips, sauce and Monterey Jack cheese. Repeat layers; top with sour cream. Bake in 350°F oven 30 minutes. Sprinkle with Cheddar cheese and bake 10 minutes longer. Let stand 15 minutes before cutting into squares.   *Makes 6 to 8 servings*

BRAZILIAN CORN AND SHRIMP MOQUECA CASSEROLE

- 2 tablespoons olive oil
- ½ cup chopped onion
- ¼ cup chopped green bell pepper
- ¼ cup tomato sauce
- 2 tablespoons chopped parsley
- ½ teaspoon TABASCO® pepper sauce
- 1 pound medium cooked shrimp
  Salt to taste
- 2 tablespoons all-purpose flour
- 1 cup milk
- 1 can (16 ounces) cream-style corn
  Grated Parmesan cheese

In large oven-proof skillet over medium-high heat, heat oil. Add onion, bell pepper, tomato sauce, parsley and TABASCO and cook, stirring occasionally, for 5 minutes. Add shrimp and salt. Cover and reduce heat to low, and simmer for 2 to 3 minutes. Preheat oven to 375°F. Sprinkle flour over shrimp mixture; stir. Add milk gradually, stirring after each addition. Cook over medium heat until mixture thickens. Remove from heat. Pour corn over mixture; do not stir. Sprinkle with Parmesan cheese. Bake for 30 minutes or until browned.   *Makes 4 servings*

CHICKEN MILANO

2 cloves garlic, minced
2 boneless skinless chicken breasts, halved
    (about 1¼ pounds)
½ teaspoon dried basil leaves, crushed
⅛ teaspoon crushed red pepper flakes
    Salt and black pepper
1 tablespoon olive oil
1 can (14½ ounces) DEL MONTE® Italian
    Style Stewed Tomatoes
1 can (16 ounces) DEL MONTE® Cut Green
    Italian Beans or Blue Lake Cut Green
    Beans, drained
¼ cup whipping cream

Rub garlic over chicken. Sprinkle with basil and red pepper. Season with salt and black pepper. In skillet, brown chicken in oil over medium-high heat. Stir in tomatoes. Cover; simmer 5 minutes. Uncover; reduce heat to medium and cook 8 to 10 minutes or until liquid is slightly thickened and chicken is tender. Stir in green beans and cream; heat through. *Do not boil.*   *Makes 4 servings*

Prep and Cook Time: 25 minutes

ORIENTAL BEEF & NOODLE TOSS

1 pound lean ground beef
2 packages (3 ounces each) Oriental flavor
    instant ramen noodles, divided
2 cups water
2 cups frozen Oriental vegetable mixture
⅛ teaspoon ground ginger
2 tablespoons thinly sliced green onion

1. In large nonstick skillet, brown ground beef over medium heat 8 to 10 minutes or until beef is no longer pink. Remove with slotted spoon; pour off drippings. Season beef with one seasoning packet from noodles; set aside.

2. In same skillet, combine water, vegetables, noodles, ginger and remaining seasoning packet. Bring to a boil; reduce heat. Cover; simmer 3 minutes or until noodles are tender, stirring occasionally.

3. Return beef to skillet; heat through. Stir in green onion before serving.   *Makes 4 servings*

*Favorite recipe from **National Live Stock & Meat Board***

Chicken Milano

INTERNATIONAL FARE

SPANISH STYLE BEEF AND RICE CASSEROLE

1¼ pounds boneless beef chuck shoulder steak, cut ¾ inch thick
1½ tablespoons olive oil
½ cup chopped green bell pepper
⅓ cup chopped onion
1 clove garlic, crushed
¾ cup uncooked rice
2 teaspoons chili powder
¾ teaspoon salt
⅛ teaspoon pepper
1 can (14½ ounces) tomatoes, undrained, broken up
¾ cup frozen peas, thawed

Cut steak into ¼-inch-wide strips; cut strips into 2-inch pieces.

Heat oven to 350°F. Heat oil in large skillet over medium-high heat 5 minutes. Cook and stir beef, bell pepper, onion and garlic 2 to 3 minutes or until beef is no longer pink; place in 2-quart casserole. Stir in rice, chili powder, salt and pepper. Add enough water to tomatoes to measure 2 cups; add to casserole. Cover tightly and bake 50 minutes or until rice is tender. Remove from oven; stir in peas. *Makes 4 servings*

Favorite recipe from **National Live Stock & Meat Board**

CHICKEN PICADILLO ENCHILADAS

1 can (16 ounces) stewed tomatoes
1½ cups PACE® Picante Sauce, divided
3 cups shredded or diced cooked chicken
1 red bell pepper, chopped
¼ cup dark raisins
¼ cup coarsely chopped, slivered toasted almonds
⅛ teaspoon cinnamon
1 garlic clove, minced
12 flour tortillas (7 to 8 inch)
1½ cups (6 ounces) shredded Monterey Jack cheese
Optional garnishes: shredded lettuce, ripe olive slices, chopped tomatoes, dairy sour cream

Combine tomatoes, ¾ cup picante sauce, chicken, bell pepper, raisins, almonds, cinnamon and garlic in large skillet. Bring to a boil; reduce heat and simmer, uncovered, 10 minutes or until most of liquid is absorbed. Spoon ⅓ cup chicken mixture into center of each tortilla. Roll tortillas; place seam side down in greased 13 × 9 × 2-inch baking dish. Spoon remaining ¾ cup picante sauce evenly over tortillas. Cover with foil. Bake at 350°F 20 minutes or until heated through. Sprinkle with cheese. Garnish as desired and serve with additional picante sauce. *Makes 6 servings*

Spanish Style Beef and Rice Casserole

MEXI-CORN LASAGNA

- 1 pound ground beef
- 1 can (17 ounces) whole kernel corn, drained
- 1 can (15 ounces) tomato sauce
- 1 cup PACE® picante sauce
- 1 tablespoon chili powder
- 1½ teaspoons ground cumin
- 1 carton (16 ounces) low fat cottage cheese
- 2 eggs, slightly beaten
- ¼ cup grated Parmesan cheese
- 1 teaspoon oregano leaves, crushed
- ½ teaspoon garlic salt
- 12 corn tortillas
- 1 cup (4 ounces) shredded Cheddar cheese

Brown meat in large skillet; drain. Add corn, tomato sauce, picante sauce, chili powder and cumin. Simmer, stirring frequently, 5 minutes. Combine cottage cheese, eggs, Parmesan cheese, oregano and garlic salt; mix well. Arrange 6 tortillas on bottom and up sides of lightly greased 13 × 9 × 2-inch baking dish, overlapping as necessary. Top with half the meat mixture. Spoon cheese mixture over meat. Arrange remaining tortillas over cheese, overlapping as necessary. Top with remaining meat mixture. Bake in preheated oven at 375°F about 30 minutes or until hot and bubbly. Remove from oven; sprinkle with Cheddar cheese. Let stand 10 minutes before serving with additional picante sauce.   *Makes 8 servings*

SCANDINAVIAN CHICKEN

- 3 tablespoons butter
- 6 boneless skinless chicken thighs, cut into 1-inch pieces
- 1 teaspoon salt
- ¼ teaspoon pepper
- ⅔ cup finely chopped onion
- 1 cup mushrooms, sliced
- ¾ cup sour cream
- ½ cup (2 ounces) shredded Havarti cheese
- ¼ cup plain fresh bread crumbs
- 2 tablespoons chopped fresh parsley

In large skillet, melt butter over medium-high heat. Add chicken; cook, stirring occasionally, about 7 minutes or until browned. Sprinkle with salt and pepper. Add onion; cook and stir until onion is tender, about 5 minutes. Add mushrooms; cook 5 minutes, stirring occasionally, until chicken is no longer pink in center. Reduce heat to low; stir in sour cream and cheese. Cook until cheese melts, about 2 minutes. Stir in bread crumbs; sprinkle with fresh parsley.   *Makes 4 servings*

Favorite recipe from National Broiler Council

Mexi-Corn Lasagna

INTERNATIONAL FARE

SAUSAGE & PASTA PRIMAVERA

4 ounces uncooked spaghetti
12 ounces beef knockwurst or beef polish
  sausage links, cut diagonally into
  ½-inch-thick slices
½ pound fresh asparagus,* trimmed, cut
  diagonally into 1-inch pieces
1 medium onion, cut lengthwise into thin
  wedges
¼ cup water
1 clove garlic, minced
2 medium tomatoes, coarsely chopped
2 tablespoons thinly sliced fresh basil**
2 tablespoons grated Parmesan cheese
  (optional)

1. Cook spaghetti according to package directions; keep warm.

2. Meanwhile in large skillet, combine beef sausage, asparagus, onion, water and garlic. Cook over medium-high heat 5 to 7 minutes or until asparagus is crisp-tender, stirring occasionally. Add spaghetti, tomatoes and basil; toss lightly. Cook 2 minutes or until heated through.

3. Serve with Parmesan cheese, if desired.

Makes 4 servings

*One package (10 ounces) thawed frozen cut asparagus may be substituted for fresh asparagus.

**1½ teaspoons dried basil leaves may be substituted for 2 tablespoons fresh basil.

Favorite recipe from **National Live Stock & Meat Board**

CHICKEN RISOTTO

¾ pound boneless skinless chicken breast,
  thinly sliced
¾ cup onion, chopped
1 tablespoon vegetable oil
2 cups uncooked instant brown rice
1 tablespoon plus 1 teaspoon sugar
1 tablespoon prepared horseradish
4 cups chicken broth
1 medium green bell pepper, sliced
1 medium red bell pepper, sliced
1 can (14 ounces) black beans, rinsed and
  drained
¼ cup grated Parmesan cheese

In large skillet, cook and stir chicken and onion in oil over high heat 5 minutes. Add rice, sugar, horseradish and broth. Reduce heat to medium. Simmer, covered, 15 minutes or until rice is tender. Add both peppers and beans. Simmer 5 minutes. Sprinkle with Parmesan cheese before serving.

Makes 4 servings

Sausage & Pasta Primavera

PAELLA A LA ESPAÑOLA

2 tablespoons margarine or butter
1¼ to 1½ pounds chicken thighs, skinned
1 package (7.2 ounces) RICE-A-RONI® Rice Pilaf
1 can (14½ or 16 ounces) tomatoes or stewed tomatoes, undrained
½ teaspoon turmeric (optional)
⅛ teaspoon hot pepper sauce or black pepper
8 ounces cooked, deveined, shelled medium shrimp
1 cup frozen peas
Lemon wedges

1. In large skillet, melt margarine over medium heat. Add chicken; cook 2 minutes on each side or until browned. Remove from skillet; set aside, reserving drippings. Keep warm.

2. In same skillet, sauté rice pilaf mix in reserved drippings over medium heat until pasta is lightly browned. Stir in 1½ cups water, tomatoes, turmeric, hot pepper sauce and contents of seasoning packet. Bring to a boil over high heat; stir in chicken.

3. Cover; reduce heat. Simmer 20 minutes. Stir in shrimp and peas.

4. Cover; continue to simmer 5 to 10 minutes or until liquid is absorbed and rice is tender. Serve with lemon wedges.   *Makes 4 servings*

CHINA CHOY QUICHE

1 unbaked (9-inch) pie shell
3 eggs
⅔ cup milk
1 (8-ounce) can LA CHOY® Sliced Water Chestnuts, drained and coarsely chopped
1 cup (4 ounces) shredded Monterey Jack cheese
¾ cup *each:* finely chopped red bell pepper and sliced fresh mushrooms
⅓ cup sliced green onions
1 tablespoon LA CHOY® Soy Sauce
½ teaspoon *each:* garlic powder and dry mustard
¼ teaspoon *each:* black pepper and Oriental sesame oil

Preheat oven to 425°F. Bake pie shell 5 minutes; set aside. *Reduce oven temperature to 350°F.* In large bowl, beat together eggs and milk; stir in remaining ingredients. Pour into partially baked shell. Bake 50 to 55 minutes or until knife inserted 1 inch from edge comes out clean. Let stand 10 minutes before serving. Garnish, if desired.

Makes 1 (9-inch) quiche

Paella a la Española

Acknowledgments

The publishers would like to thank the companies and organizations listed below for the use of their recipes and photographs in this publication.

American Celery Council

Blue Diamond Growers

Borden Kitchens, Borden, Inc.

California Table Grape Commission

Canned Food Information Council

Colorado Potato Administrative
    Committee

Chef Paul Prudhomme's Magic
    Seasoning Blends™

The Creamette Company

Cucina Classica Italiana, Inc.

Del Monte Corporation

Dole Food Company, Inc.

Florida Department of Agriculture
    and Consumer Services Bureau of
    Seafood and Aquaculture

Golden Grain/Mission Pasta

Heinz U.S.A.

Hunt Food Co.

Kraft Foods, Inc.

Lawry's® Foods, Inc.

Thomas J. Lipton Co.

Louis Rich Company

McCormick & Co., Inc.

McIlhenny Company

Minnesota Cultivated Wild Rice
    Council

Nabisco Foods Group

National Broiler Council

National Dairy Board

National Live Stock & Meat Board

Newman's Own, Inc.

North Dakota Wheat Commission

Pace Foods, Ltd.

The Procter & Gamble Company

Reckitt & Colman Inc.

Riviana Foods Inc.

Southeast United Dairy Industry
    Association, Inc.

StarKist Seafood Company

USA Dry Pea and Lentil Council

USA Rice Council

Wisconsin Milk Marketing Board

— Index —

METRIC CONVERSION CHART

VOLUME MEASUREMENTS (dry)

⅛ teaspoon = 0.5 mL
¼ teaspoon = 1 mL
½ teaspoon = 2 mL
¾ teaspoon = 4 mL
1 teaspoon = 5 mL
1 tablespoon = 15 mL
2 tablespoons = 30 mL
¼ cup = 60 mL
⅓ cup = 75 mL
½ cup = 125 mL
⅔ cup = 150 mL
¾ cup = 175 mL
1 cup = 250 mL
2 cups = 1 pint = 500 mL
3 cups = 750 mL
4 cups = 1 quart = 1 L

VOLUME MEASUREMENTS (fluid)

1 fluid ounce (2 tablespoons) = 30 mL
4 fluid ounces (½ cup) = 125 mL
8 fluid ounces (1 cup) = 250 mL
12 fluid ounces (1½ cups) = 375 mL
16 fluid ounces (2 cups) = 500 mL

WEIGHTS (mass)

½ ounce = 15 g
1 ounce = 30 g
3 ounces = 90 g
4 ounces = 120 g
8 ounces = 225 g
10 ounces = 285 g
12 ounces = 360 g
16 ounces = 1 pound = 450 g

DIMENSIONS

$\frac{1}{16}$ inch = 2 mm
⅛ inch = 3 mm
¼ inch = 6 mm
½ inch = 1.5 cm
¾ inch = 2 cm
1 inch = 2.5 cm

OVEN TEMPERATURES

250°F = 120°C
275°F = 140°C
300°F = 150°C
325°F = 160°C
350°F = 180°C
375°F = 190°C
400°F = 200°C
425°F = 220°C
450°F = 230°C

BAKING PAN SIZES

Utensil	Size in Inches/Quarts	Metric Volume	Size in Centimeters
Baking or Cake Pan (square or rectangular)	8×8×2	2 L	20×20×5
	9×9×2	2.5 L	22×22×5
	12×8×2	3 L	30×20×5
	13×9×2	3.5 L	33×23×5
Loaf Pan	8×4×3	1.5 L	20×10×7
	9×5×3	2 L	23×13×7
Round Layer Cake Pan	8×1½	1.2 L	20×4
	9×1½	1.5 L	23×4
Pie Plate	8×1¼	750 mL	20×3
	9×1¼	1 L	23×3
Baking Dish or Casserole	1 quart	1 L	—
	1½ quart	1.5 L	—
	2 quart	2 L	—